WITHDRAWN

Aspects of modern sociology

Social processes

GENERAL EDITORS

John Barron Mays
Eleanor Rathbone Professor of Sociology, University of Liverpool

Maurice Craft
Goldsmiths' Professor of Education, University of London

Social Change

Social theory and historical processes

Anthony D. Smith B.A., M.Sc., Ph.D.

Lecturer in Comparative Sociology
University of Reading

Longman

London and New York

Longman Group Limited
London

*Associated companies, branches and representatives through-
out the world*
Published in the United States by Longman Inc., New York

First published 1976

ISBN 0582 48010.8 cased
            48011.6 paper

Set in IBM Century
by Type Practitioners Ltd, Sevenoaks, Kent
and printed in England
by Lowe & Brydone Ltd, Thetford, Norfolk

Library of Congress Cataloguing in Publication Data

Smith, Anthony David; 1939—Social change.

(Aspects of modern sociology : social processes)
Bibliography: p.
1. Social change.   2.   Social history. I. Title.
HM101.S643   301.24   75-42477
ISBN 0-582-48010-8
ISBN 0-582-48011-6 pbk.

Contents

Contents

Editors' preface

The first series in Longman's *Aspects of Modern Sociology* library was concerned with the social structure of modern Britain, and was intended for students following professional and other courses in universities, polytechnics, colleges of education, and elsewhere in further and higher education, as well as for those members of a wider public wishing to pursue an interest in the nature and structure of British society.

A further series set out to examine the history, aims, techniques and limitations of social research; and this third series is concerned with a number of fundamental social processes. The presentation in each case is basically analytical, but each title will also seek to embody a particular viewpoint. It is hoped that these very relevant introductory texts will also prove to be of interest to a wider, lay readership as well as to students in higher education.

JOHN BARRON MAYS
MAURICE CRAFT

Acknowledgements

In a general work of this kind, one's intellectual debts are manifold. I should however like to single out the important work of Professors S.N. Eisenstadt, W.E. Moore and R.A. Nisbet in clarifying the central issues of social development and diffusion. I should also like to thank Dr Herminio Martins for letting me have a copy of his illuminating paper 'Time and theory in sociology' before publication.

I should like to record my thanks to the series Editors, Professor J.B. Mays and Professor M. Craft, for asking me to contribute this volume to their series on *Social Processes*. Responsibility for the views expressed, as well as for errors and omissions, is naturally mine alone.

A.D. SMITH
London, September 1975

1 The nature of change

My aim in this book is to consider some problems and issues in the field of historical change. Change comes in so many forms and rates, and is so pervasive a phenomenon in social life, that one may well question the need for a special study of 'social change' within the social sciences. I hope, nevertheless, to show that there is a sound case for such a study, so long as it confines itself to certain problems about the origins, mechanisms and forms of change. These problems find their classic expression in some of the main theories of social change, and it is for this reason, that the major part of this book examines the relationship between these theories and various kinds of historical processes. The emphasis throughout is on the utility of such theories in accounting for different sequences of events as these appear in our historical records. That is why the problems of exogenous impact and voluntaristic innovation receive considerable attention, since they bring into sharp focus the difficulties encountered in relating various levels of historical changes to one another.

No attempt has been made to be comprehensive in dealing with the many theories of change that have been advanced in the last two centuries. There are many excellent readers and accounts of such theories, many of which have little bearing on problems of the origins and forms of actual historical changes. Nor have I attempted to add yet another 'theory' of change to the existing stock, believing such efforts to be largely misplaced. Instead, I have proceeded on the basis of a belief in the need for an historical sociology of change, and have selected and evaluated certain theories in the light of this criterion, holding that in this complex field approaches and perspectives are more valuable than overall frameworks or theories.

The ideal of change

In the last two centuries change has been so rapid and pervasive that one can easily be persuaded that it is the 'stuff of life', that society like nature is in a state of ceaseless flux, and that change rather than persistence is the normal and natural condition of life. If anything, change seems to be accelerating. If we contrast the social climate of Britain in the late 1950s with that of the early 1970s, the debates about nuclear disarmament, the Cold War, comprehensive schools or rock music seems faintly antiquated in an era of oil and energy crisis, inflation and terrorism. We no longer count even in terms of generations when we recognise considerable changes in such phenomena as economic curves, international climates, educational debates, social problems or artistic styles. 'Eras', or at any rate periods, seem to undergo significant shifts every ten or fifteen years. A new climate and different concerns emerge, pushing aside older generations who never quite enjoy the fullness of experience, the savour of their era, as did earlier generations. Age itself is devalued, and youth is equated with the vigour of change, dynamic activity and renewal, with hope of real improvement amid so much disillusion. So that in the end change itself becomes the pre-eminent value, the goal of all effort, and stability is seen as immobility or reaction, a refuge for the old and disappointed.

This fundamental contrast between the yearning for an old but decayed order, and the messianic brashness of novelty and advance, divides not just generations but also whole cultures and culture areas. The nostalgic hankering for imperial greatness, for Edwardian manners or Art Nouveau, the revival of interest in the gay abandon and Art Deco of the 'twenties

2

and 'thirties, despite unemployment and threats of war, appeal not only to older generations who recall their youth, but to older cultures like Britain, or those who are reacting against too rapid a pace of change, as in America.[1] The turbulence of earlier decades is transmuted into a gilded stability, in which codes of conduct and proprieties of status were duly observed, in contrast to the grey confusion and unbridled sectionalism of the present. In the new states outside Europe, there is an equally vehement rejection of previous eras as archaic, hierarchical and oppressive, by younger generations bent on enjoying expanded opportunities and imbued with ideals and myths of nation-building and the Great Leap Forward. As makers of history they try to postpone their own absorption into history, fearful that their present changes will become future stabilities, against which in turn others will revolt.

Hence change and the sense of transience of all phenomena, however firmly rooted they seem, have become the overriding experiences and values of our century, even among those who long for a return to their vision of a better, more ordered, more spacious and enduring era. Their very sense of loss attests the predominant role of change in the modern social consciousness.

This all-pervading sense of change has also affected the climate of social theory and social research in the last decade. For nearly forty years after the First World War many sociologists were content to explore the workings of particular social structures and renounce the search for 'laws' of their social development, which had characterised the work of their nineteenth-century predecessors. Since the late 1950s, however, interest in the forms and characteristics of 'structural change' has revived. The properties of social systems, formerly conceived in fairly static terms, have come to be treated as dynamic social processes. Likewise, the emphasis on a tightly knit interdependence of parts within a social system has given way to looser constructs which allow more variation among the parts and therefore a more 'dynamic' equilibrium among their roles and institutions.[2]

Empirically, too, the 1960s witnessed a much livelier concern with issues of change and development. The most controversial and important revolved around the status and prospects of 'development' and revolution in the Third World. This in turn bred an interest in such related topics as aid, exploitation, urbanisation, neocolonialism, nationalism, military rule and westernisation, topics which obviously demand a broader comparative approach and greater regard for sequences and processes over time. The study of non-European areas led to reappraisals of European developments, with Weber's problem of the role and peculiarities of Western civilisation being reformulated in more comparative economic and political terms. There have also been more historical studies of vital topics like race, empires, peasants, sects and revolutions.

All this adds up to a new climate of social investigation and theorising, in which the creation of a genuinely historical sociology becomes a paramount aim. In some cases contact with the aims and methods of historians has been minimised to the incorporation of a greater array of historical data into preconceived schemes of social change. But in others, there has been a deeper and more intensive attempt to bring the two disciplines into harmony and coherence by greater study of the methods of history. The net result is that most branches of social theory and investigation have paid more attention to the historical record in the last decade, and few have been altogether immune from the sort of comparisons which entail an appeal to historical data.[3]

Change and stability

So pervasive in our experience, so important in our scale of values has change become, both in the general social consciousness and in recent scholarly research, that many would regard the study of social life and that of social change as coextensive. Sociology, in particular, is seen as nothing more or less than the study of social change in all its forms. And the study of social persistence must, in that case, become merely a special case of the study of social change, namely arrested change.

This seems to me to present too sweeping and misleading a view of the scope and purposes of a study of 'social change'. It rests on three dubious assumptions. The first is that history is flux, and social change must therefore be an essential component of all social life, and its natural property. The second follows from this, to assert that either stability and persistence of flux and change must be both logically and substantively prior, and therefore the study of persistence must be simply a special case of the study of change. The final assumption is more empirical. It asserts that the main characteristics of the modern period or generations are valid for the past, and hence that change has always been ubiquitous and natural in human affairs.

Now it is true that movement and activity are universal attributes of social life. Social groups and organisations always manifest a myriad small-scale activites and movements, and even beliefs and styles are subject to many minor shifts in expression over a longer period. Fashions, business activity and crime rates are full of minor fluctuations, as are the relations between members of small groups like families or clubs. And motion is an attribute of change, since the latter always involves some kind of shift from one state of affairs to another.

But change is not simply motion or activity. It involves other attributes, which designate alteration and rearrangement. There can be many movements and ceaseless activity, but no real change within or between units. This is partly a matter of decision about what constitutes 'significant' change and what quite trivial and repetitive activity; but to assert that change is natural, an immanent property of social life, purely on the basis of such miniscule movements, is to trivialise an important issue and reject the commonsense notion of change as involving significant rearrangements and modifications. The course of the river must alter, not merely its waters.[4]

There is of course another, deeper sense in which all history is flux, that is, irregular, inconstant, changeable. But this condition may be the precipitant of the interaction of many separate units and patterns, not a property of social structures or social life as such. Change may therefore be neither essential or natural, but only usual and 'normal' in so far as it is a function of the multiplicity of units.

But so, it appears, is persistence. And this fact casts doubt on the second assumption, namely that change (and its study) must logically *and* substantively precede social persistence and stability, the latter being treated simply as cases of 'arrested change'. No doubt, many stable orders and persisting patterns originate as cases of a slowing down of the rate of change to the point of minimal movement and shift. Weber's example of the routinisation of charisma springs to mind; so do such institutions as caste in India and feudal estates in Japan and medieval Europe.[5] But, however originated, these institutions display remarkable durability; like the forms of Egyptian art or Byzantine ritual, they set the limits within which for centuries men and women, in different social positions, were compelled to live and act, with only prescribed deviations and minor modifications. In our own societies, whether we consider the macro-level of the nation-state or the micro-level of the family and neighbourhood, routine, repetition, tradition and prescribed behaviour are almost as important a part of social and political life as the many changes in technology, attitudes and life styles that we encounter. On a substantive level, therefore, it is extremely difficult to judge the priority of either persistence or change in social affairs. And similarly with social attitudes; change may today be a dominant concern of many people, but social conservatism remains a powerful force, and not merely in rural areas. People continue to cling to their conceptions and modes of behaviour, even when the conditions which fostered them have long since disappeared. One has only to think of the continuing deference of some workers today in societies once ruled by landed aristocracies, or the persistence of ritual and magic in new states undergoing considerable westernisation.

I am not suggesting that persistence and stability are any more the natural or normal condition of social life than change and flux. Nothing in the historical record, it seems to me, requires us to regard either as substantively precedent. There is, however, a case for arguing the *logical* priority of persistence over change. Change is always predicated of a pattern or object: something undergoes change, even if that something is utterly destroyed and replaced by something else. It is always in relation to some entity or state of affairs that we speak of change. Hence it follows that as a matter of method we must start our investigation from a given pattern, unit or object, and persistence must therefore be accorded methodological, but not substantive priority.

Enough has already been said to cast doubt on the third assumption about the ubiquity and naturalness of change throughout history. In fact, the modern era since the French Revolution is atypical. It is not simply that the rate of change in the last two centuries is so much faster than in previous epochs. It is also more massive, pervasive, irregular and disturbing for nations and individuals; and as Moore points out, change today has consequences that often reverberate throughout the area or even the globe, there is a far higher proportion of planned change than before, and as we saw, people tend to expect change as an everday occurrence.[6]

Of course, traditional societies have also undergone considerable changes. This is not only the case with well documented civilisations like Rome or China, but also holds for lesser tribes and cultures about which we possess less evidence. Only the most isolated tribes have managed to retain their customs, attitudes and social organisation with relatively little rearrangement and alteration over long periods. But few have succeeded in remaining untouched by outside influences or changes in their environment.[7]

Despite this evidence of change in premodern societies, there does appear to be a fundamental difference in the respective proportions and importance of change and stability as between even complex traditional and modern, industrial societies. It is only in the latter that we can safely argue the substantive predominance of change; and even here massive changes have left many attitudes and forms of behaviour intact from generation to generation, from laws and constitutions to styles of cooking and fashions.[8]

In this respect, therefore, as in many others, the modern age does not exemplify previous eras; and we may not infer the historical ubiquity of change from its present striking predominance.

The qualities of change

If change is not a natural constituent of all social life, if stability and persistence are as vital as change and flux, and if the present near-ubiquity of change is atypical, then how shall we conceive of social change and its study?

Rather than proceed immediately to the problem of definition, I shall seek to delimit the field by enumerating some of the qualities of change. The first of these arises from a point already mentioned, namely, that change is a predicate of subjects. Change is always change of some pattern or thing, be it a constitution or a coat, capitalism or civilisation. (There is an important distinction here, to which I return in the next chapter, in regard to transitive and intransitive uses of the verb, but it does not affect the present argument.) In the social world, such subjects are generally traits, patterns or units. Anthropologists and archaeologists have usually concerned themselves with traits, their provenance, antiquity and

significance. For sociologists and historians, it is patterns or *NB*
units, sometimes called 'configurations' or 'constellations',
which form the subject of their investigations. A unit may be
seen as an aggregate of related patterns, which may range
from mere temporal juxtaposition to relations of close interdependence between the patterns. In other words, we should
not prejudge the type and proximity of relationship between
patterns in referring to such units. Examples of the latter
would be churches, firms, neighbourhoods, nations, states,
nuclear and extended families, cities and civilisations. As this
random list shows, the type and degree of relationship between the constituent patterns varies considerably.

Patterns themselves divide into two main groups. The first
are constituted of norms and rules, customary or prescribed,
which in some measure govern behaviour. So modes of cooking and eating in different cultures, of etiquette and dress,
follow certain customary prescriptions and issue in patterns
which are more or less easily recognisable. Similarly with
larger and more openly prescribed patterns of speech or
political activity, which are governed by rules of language and
laws. But there is also another use of the term 'pattern', as
when we refer to the pattern of trade or colonisation, conquest or revolution. Here the element of rule-governed behaviour is less important (though there may be a proportion,
as for example in different types of colonial regime) than the
tracing of a typical sequence of events. In other words, terms
like colonisation or revolution sum up, for all their specific
qualities in particular situations, a set of related events forming a pattern which we recognise by that term as recurrent
chains and sequences in history. Alongside many unique
attributes, there are also certain general ones deriving from
the placing of certain events in temporal and spatial relations,
which therefore justify the generic term.

What this implies is that change as the predicate of a subject is always *spatial* as well as temporal. That is, it is concerned with subjects situated in space, physical or social. The

patterns and units which change (or are changed) vary in size, scale, depth and location in relation to different populations. They share however the quality of contact (in varying degrees) with other patterns or units situated in space; and it is this quality of spatial juxtaposition which is essential for the subsequent analysis of change.

The second quality of change, its *temporal* character, is as vital and more obvious. The implications are, however, sometimes overlooked. The first is that change must not be confused with simple variation. Variation of forms and structures is, again, univeral in history; but a statement of coexisting differences within or between units does not amount to a statement that something has changed. A glance at the political map of medieval Europe reveals all manner of entities—free cities, orders of knights, principalities and duchies, kingdoms, papal domains, empires—coexisting and interacting; but such variety does not in itself amount to change.[9] The second implication is more important for the analysis of change. If change is always change of patterns and units in a particular space and time, then we encounter special difficulties in comparing similar phenomena located in, say, different centuries (as well as continents). Many such phenomena, like empires, millennialisms or ethnic conflicts, have invited comparative analysis. But if the time factor is crucial, then there are obvious difficulties in comparing common patterns in Hammurabi's and Harun al Rashid's empires, or the French Revolution with the Chinese Communist.[10]

Temporality also carried with it another correlate of change which I have mentioned, *motion*. Before it was said that motion or movement in itself does not amount to change. As against this, we must add that change is inconceivable without movement, and this carries the further implication of dynamic activity inherent in our concept of change. Although such activity does not in itself specify change, it does provide a rough and ready sign and symptom of its possibility.

10

A fourth quality, the relation of change to *events*, is much less obvious. Events in themselves do not constitute change, nor do they necessarily lead to change. On the other hand, change always involves some reference to events, some turning-points or occurrences which mark a point of transition. Usually, more than one such event is involved: a whole series of events led up to the civil war between Caesar and Pompey, not just the crossing of the Rubicon. Quite often, the events simply initiate a process: the founding of a dynasty may lead to the growth of an army and a bureaucracy which later provide the focus of a nation, as in Prussia, or colonial conquest and exploitation may induce rapid urbanisation as in Zambia or Nigeria. These processes are composed of recurrent events, like recruitment and rule-making activities in armies and bureaucracies, or acts of migration and re-employment of thousands of individuals in the process or urbanisation. Such recurrent events are, however, rather different in nature from the once-for-all events of colonisation or dynasty-founding, since in the former the turning-point results from some degree of cumulation for the larger entity, even where for the smaller, the individual who is recruited or who migrates, those acts or events constitute turning-points in his or her life. This distinction will be elaborated later; for the present it suffices to note the event-referring quality of social change.

The final aspect of change to which I wish to draw attention is its connotation of real *difference* as between patterns (or more rarely units). Change is not change until the motion of patterns in time and space has resulted in another pattern or at any rate another form for that pattern. Again, this is a matter for judgment in specific instances, as to whether we can speak of a 'genuine' or 'significant' change having occurred. But, in general, change implies alteration, the exchange of one pattern for another, one form for another, as the etymology suggests. Or we may rephrase this by positing an ideal-type of change, in which the existing pattern gives way to another, but admit lesser changes deviating from this ideal as

11

modifications of the existing pattern.

The five qualities I have enumerated, that change consists in temporal, event-referring, motion of spatial patterns resulting in clear difference from the preceding pattern (or state of patterns), point to an important general conclusion. This is that social change is pre-eminently *historical* in nature, that it is essentially concerned with sequences of events and movements in space and time; and hence that change cannot be studied apart from the historical record, which indeed must form the starting-point of every investigation in this field. This conclusion might seem obvious, were it not for the fact that for some decades many sociologists have disregarded its implications, preferring to oppose social change to historical sequences. If my argument is correct, such a disjunction is no longer acceptable, with important consequences for our choice of concepts and models in the analysis of change. This is a topic to which I return in chapter 4.

The definition of change

Definitions are judged by their utility, and one may legitimately question the usefulness of any attempt to define so vast and varied a phenomenon as social or historical change. Nevertheless, in so far as it has been my aim in this chapter to delimit the field of social change from that of persistence, a brief consideration of a few definitions may provide further clarification.

We may start from the notion that change is a succession of temporal differences between and within units. This is very close to the definition given by Nisbet in his important critique of the idea of social growth, *Social Change and History*. 'Change', he writes, 'we may define as *a succession of differences in time within a persisting identity*' (his italics).[1] Both definitions are broad; but Nisbet tends to emphasise the continuing identity of the subject undergoing change, in

12

accordance with his belief that persistence and fixity substantively as well as logically precede change. This leads him perhaps to neglect the important case of destruction of patterns or units and their replacement by completely different ones. An example would be the collapse of the Roman empire and its replacement in the West by tribal kingdoms after AD 476. Change has obviously occurred here, although we can only predicate it of a geographical area and set of populations, not of the Roman Empire. Since the breakdown of units and patterns constitutes an important case, we cannot lay so much emphasis on the persistence and identity of a given unit in our definition. Hence the phrase 'between and within units' in the first definition.

For much change, this is undoubtedly an acceptable formulation. But it fails to distinguish between repetitive cycles like the round of the week, the seasons or the life-cycle, and non-repetitive alterations in the direction of patterns and trends. It also fails to catch the dynamic movement of change and its involvement with critical turning-points and decisive occurrences. This is even true of attempts to define change in terms of new directions within and between patterns and units. Novelty is an important element in all non-repetitive or cyclical change, even in a scheme like Pareto's cyclical alternation of elites.[1][2] But the novelty of change is a product of events, which divert the pattern or unit from its course in a decisive and often sudden manner, and involve its movement from one condition to another.

For these reasons, I would prefer to define change as *a succession of events which produce over time a modification or replacement of particular patterns or units by other novel ones*. This places events at the centre of our analysis of change mechanisms, and at the same time allows for partial as well as total substitution of either the patterns or the units which are alleged to change. It includes therefore all stages of change, from simple piecemeal reform through radical reform and then revolution to the ultimate case of breakdown-cum-emergence, i.e. the destruction of the unit and its replacement by a new type of unit (or several of that type).[1][3]

This definition allows us to delimit a field of study, which, while not isolated from other fields of social sciences, possesses its own specific problems and procedures. The burden of analysis in this field falls, according to this definition, on the conditions and types of event which produce alterations, and on the forms which those alterations (whether modifications or substitutions) take. Put differently, any analysis of social change which is genuinely historical must attend to three sorts of question: how did the change originate, by what mechanisms did the events produce the change, and what form did its effects take in the pattern or unit under consideration? In other words, analyses of historical change must consider the three problems of the sources, channels of diffusion and repercussions of change for the pattern or unit undergoing change. The degree to which different models and theories of change measure up to the requirements posed by the three aspects, and the extent to which they consider all three problems, is an important test of their efficacy and utility. More generally, the degree to which they make a serious attempt to come to grips with the sources, mechanisms and forms of social change—the peculiar problems in this field—must form the basis for any judgment of their merits as theories of social change.

2 Varieties of change

A conception which equates social with historical change faces immediately the problem that histories are multiple and the forms of change numerous. The kinds of historical change deemed significant by each investigator depend on certain assumptions regarding the relation of patterns and units to chronological time; the analytic 'region' or 'sector' of pattern or unit in which the change is situated; the mode by which event sequences are translated into pattern modifications and substitutions.

In this chapter I look at some key distinctions between types of historical change in terms of these criteria and problem areas, distinctions which enable us to locate and assess the value of different models and theories in accounting for the origins, channels and forms of social change.

Events, processes and trends

One of the commonest distinctions in the study of change is that between changes *within* and *of* a structure or system. First formulated by Radcliffe-Brown, it can be applied as much to behaviour patterns or codes as to different kinds of unit.[1] The American Constitution, for example, despite several amendments, retains its characteristic form or pattern; but were future amendments to overturn its underlying principle of 'checks and balances', we would be justified in viewing the ensuing constitution as a new product, a change *of* the code. Similarly with changes within and of units like the

15

Vatican or Russia: the reforms of the former are 'intra-systemic', while the October Revolution in Russia changed its whole structure. There is also the further case, already mentioned, of complete replacement of the system or unit; we may regard this case as one pole of a continuum, the other being small-scale, piecemeal reform.

For many purposes, such a rough and ready division is adequate, although in practice there is considerable blurring in the middle ranges. But it does suffer from the defect of its functionalist formulation, namely, a tendency to assume too great an interdependence of the roles and institutions composing a given unit or 'system'. It also avoids all reference to time spans and sequences of events, dealing only with the spatial component of change. Finally, and most important, its utility does tend to depend on the implicit assumption that one can specify the 'central features' of the structure of the pattern or unit and oppose significant changes in these elements to mere fluctuations or peripherally located changes.[2]

In view of these difficulties, we might reformulate the distinction by closer reference to chronological time, the base line of historical research. For every time-span or date-class chosen, there is an appropriate amount and kind of information which can be obtained. If, for example, we chose to study the rise of the Bolsheviks to power in October 1917 by analysing the sequences of events in that year alone, we gain immeasurably in detail, but also lose a more general synoptic view with its appropirate information; and if we do move to the level of decades or generations, we lose information about specific happenings—intrigues, local events, rumour, factions, personalities—which led up to the change under investigation. If we go further and analyse the Bolshevik revolution in the light of Russia's relations with the West from the time of Peter or even Ivan, or of its heritage of 'oriental despotism' or 'feudaloid' mode of production, we again gain understanding of longeval sequences at the expense of 'micro-events' which fill the pages of those who limit their descriptions to shorter time-spans.

Such examples broach a threefold classification of temporal sequences (and hence of the scope of changes) in terms of calendar events, medium-term 'processes' and long-term 'trends'. Under 'evential' change, the researcher confines himself to the detailed analysis of archival records, to the day-to-day, or at any rate, month-to-month, relationships between individuals and groups which generate and compose particular pattern substitutions. This is the characteristic approach of political, diplomatic and military history, backed today by a battery of instantaneous social survey data, such as electoral or consumer preferences, and supplemented by a great deal of social history information culled from parish records and local government reports. There are no logical criteria for fixing the lower or upper limits of this kind of 'micro-analysis', but in practice (and depending on the density of dates and happenings in a period) anything from a week to a decade can be bracketed in evential historiography.[3]

Under the heading of 'process', we can include what Braudel calls 'conjunctures', that is, sequences of intermediate duration, such as conquest or colonisation, trade relations and social movements, urbanisation and migrations, in fact all those critical 'events' (themselves composed of many events) or occurrences, with which a sociological history (or historical sociology) would be most concerned.[4]

The term 'process' refers here to typical clusters and sequences of events, that is, the second of the two senses of 'pattern' which were distinguished in the last chapter. Such sequences are generally measured in decade spans, or thereabouts; 'processual' change therefore has nothing in common with the functionalist meaning of that term, which signifies an internal property of a social system whose parts are in constant and cumulative motion.[5]

Finally we come to long-term 'trends', ranging from centuries to millennia, even hundreds of millennia, and including what are often called 'structural' changes, as well as geosocial ones. Examples of the former are the disintegration of the Roman Empire, the spread of Buddhism or Christianity, and the rise of capitalism or Renaissance humanism, while geosocial trends range from the Neolithic 'revolution' to the emergence of Australopithecines and *homo sapiens.*[6] Change here is apparently 'silent' and 'invisible', change of the largest and most enduring structures, and as such of the greatest interest to many sociologists. Indeed, those who would treat persistence as a branch of the study of change, would include automatically every large-scale structure—politics, cultural systems, modes of production—even though this formulation assumes what has often to be proved, namely, that such structures or systems are indeed undergoing trendlike changes as an essential property of their functioning. The term 'trends' is preferable to Braudel's 'structures' to signify longeval changes; for sociologists, 'structure' possesses the Durkheimian attributes of generality, endurance and constraint, which are more apposite of the study of persistence than of change. What falls within the latter's province is the rise and fall of such structures, and their replacement by others.

Classifying changes according to time-span is necessarily an approximate procedure. It does, however, highlight the centrality of 'processual' changes, which are sometimes ignored in the controversies of structuralists and interactionists. But it is exactly this medium-duration type of change which is historically crucial, both in its own right and as a bridge between micro-events and longeval trends.

Two further points are worth noting in connection with this classification. First, it remains bound to the chronological time scale and constitutes therefore as much a hierarchy of periodising as a typology. This is in accord with our view of change as essentially historical, event-related pattern substitution. It is true that the chronological scale is less useful in some areas of historical research than others and that some

18

phenomena possess their own temporal rhythms and periods. Just as histories are multiple, so are times plural; and each phenomenon, each pattern or unit, has its own chronology, bearing little relation to that of other patterns or units. The argument applies most in the field of culture history. An artistic style like the Baroque constitutes its own form and sequence of time, whether in music, architecture or painting; and this form has apparently more significance than the common location of Baroque styles in the seventeenth century in certain states of western and central Europe, a contingent fact without theoretical significance.

Taken to its logical conclusion, this argument would destroy any rationale for a truly comparative history, let alone an historical sociology. Achronological cultural relativism is just as destructive of the enterprise of historical sociology as the historian's cult of the unique period, for it denies the possibility that events and processes are interrelated, and grants an autonomy to sectors or regions of life which their common human reference and their spatial and temporal proximity must limit.[7] In the example cited above, to start from the assumption that it cannot be purely fortuitous that Baroque styles developed in a period of Catholic counter-reformation and the emergence of absolutist courts, seems more fruitful than to view these styles as separate entities subject to development only through internal structural potentialities.[8]

This leads to the second point. If the sociological enterprise hinges partly on the assumption of the possibility of the interrelatedness of events, then events and clusters or sequences of them remain the decisive referents in any classification of social changes. This does not entail the reduction of trends and processes to the level of micro-events; in practice, at any rate, methodological eventialism is unnecessary. What it does imply is that processes and even trends not only comprise events, crises, turning-points en route, but should be treated as long-range events whose interrelatedness with other processual or trend-like events is being posited. After all, events are not only the micro-events of archival historiography or clock-time; 1066, the Black Death, the Great War, the French Revolution, the Vietnam conflict, Impressionism in Paris, the Romantic movement, may all be (and have been) treated as large-scale events when viewed from a long enough perspective. It is the nature and length of the time-span itself which partly determines whether we shall view particular phenomena as events in their own right.

Regions of change

The fact that serious arguments can be brought to show that some phenomena of change possess considerable autonomy and potential suggests another criterion for classifying the great variety of changes. That criterion we may call 'region' or 'sector' of change, and it refers not to the source of change, but to the type of pattern or unit (or sphere of the unit) undergoing change.

Broadly speaking, we may distinguish three such regions: socio-economic, political and cultural. Each has its distinctive problems and forms of change, even though there may be close relations at a given time between changes in one region and those in another. The importance of the distinction resides in the possibility of asynchronous changes, where the different sectors undergo separate rates, intensities and forms of change. There is also the interesting case, where change in one or two sectors is intense and rapid, whereas in the third it is barely discernible, a pattern often found in revolutionary situations. Another idea behind the regional taxonomy is that the three sectors possess distinctive mechanisms which react differentially to a common stimulus of change, creating wholly different repercussions in the patterns or units comprising that sector.

By socio-economic change is meant changes in the patterns of resource allocation, production and interests of various groups. The social component covers also the distribution of prestige in so far as it is conditioned by property and class position. From the standpoint of historical sociology, the central issues in this region concern the emergence and decline of different functions and strata, the distribution of wealth and its fluctuations and trends, and the conflict of interest groups and classes over scarce resources. Not all of these changes are of the trend or processual kind. Micro-events may be involved in sudden market fluctuations (the Great Crash), disruption of trade patterns, the impact of technological innovations, legal enactments concerning wealth redistribution, and the discovery of scarce mineral resources. But most of the interesting changes in this region are longer-term, partly because of the close relationship with the environment and technology, and partly because of the difficulties of communications and the organisation of interest groups, strata and classes, who are often inchoate and scattered, like the gentry or peasantry.[9]

Political changes include the distribution of power and authority, the formulation of public policy and the institutionalisation of power in organisations. It does not seem profitable to separate military from other kinds of power, since there is a continuum of power from the actual use of force to subtle kinds of persuasion, and the military may often be regarded as a branch of the power hierarchy in any society, specially in empires and kingdoms, but also in both communist and western states.[10]

In treating the political region as relatively autonomous, the classification indicates the important role of organisation and the command chain in mediating stimuli of change, and in controlling their diffusion and repercussions on the pattern or units concerned. In fact, the radicalism of some present regimes should not obscure the essentially conservative nature of the political region in regard to changes. While planned change is not peculiar to the modern era, its scope and intensity have changed; though even today, that radicalism is sometimes exaggerated and its motives misconstrued. Political intelligentsias in Asian and African states have sometimes inaugurated important programmes of planned change, but the effect of their activities has been as much to control external disruptive change as to dismantle traditional institutions.[11]

The cultural sphere or region is probably the most autonomous, yet also the most pervasive. The term covers several sets of patterns—knowledge and techniques, artistic and literary styles and fashions, ideas and beliefs, and more generally artefacts and modes of customary behaviour and rituals.[12] It includes all layers of communication and style—the Great as well as the Little traditions, 'mass' as well as 'high' culture. Despite these divisions and range of variation, there is often a good deal of mutual influence between the products (artefacts, conceptions, techniques and rituals) of individuals who constitute a group; so much so that we can point with relative ease to particular ethnic or national cultures. In respect of autonomy, we must distinguish content from style in every pattern: the former tends to be more susceptible to changes in patterns in other regions, whereas style is relatively impervious to change in non-cultural patterns, though perhaps not quite as archetypically fixed as Kroeber argues in connection with artistic styles. For both at the inception and later in the course of that style's development, outside factors influence what Kroeber calls the 'choices' and 'commitments' that any art must make as it rises from initial obscurity, quite apart from more material considerations of patronage and media resources.[13]

Regional classifications contain, as I said, a prototheoretical position, in this case that the region in which changes occur is to a considerable extent isolated, self-contained and change-influencing. It says nothing about the source of change, and little about the mechanisms of its diffusion, except perhaps in the case of the political region. It is easy to confuse the three problems, since many theories of cultural or economic change have attempted to *explain* changes in the economic or cultural sectors by reference to economic or cultural factors alone (or almost alone). But an *identification* of the region of change must not be confused with a *theory* of changes in that region, even if the theory posits changes, asynchronous or simultaneous, in all regions, and locates the sources of those changes in all the regions, as the functionalists tend to do. The regional classification still retains its utility in these cases, because of the differential impact of single- or multiple-source change, on those regions affected by that stimulus. Regions are not equally vulnerable or immune to different sorts of change stimulus.

Active and passive change

Perhaps the most fundamental of all distinctions in the field of social change is that between 'active' and 'passive' modes of change. In defining change, we referred to sequences of events producing over time pattern modifications, or substitutions of new patterns, but nothing was said of the source of the events nor of the manner by which they effected substitutions, nor of the repertoire of pattern replacements. All three areas of change—sources, channels and repertoires of forms—can be differentiated according to the peculiar mode appropriate to the presence or absence of human intervention at each of the points along the chain leading to change. In other words, changes can be differentiated according to whether or not human beings actively intervene in initiating the events, in providing the channels of their impact, and in furnishing novel forms for embodying the changes.

This distinction follows from the two modes of the verb, to change, the transitive and intransitive. Macrosociology has been mainly concerned with the latter type, where modes of production, institutions, empires and nations, even civilisations, are held to change, as it were of their own accord. The analysis takes the form of enquiry into changes in a subject,

23

usually following the before-and-after model. Discussions of the 1789 Revolution take France as the subject of change, and compare her states before and after the transition of the Revolution. Similarly, the state of 'India' may be compared before and after the intervention, impact, transition or 'hump' of British colonialism; or the state of the Mediterranean world before and after the rise of Christianity.

All these examples make implicit reference to human activity, but their emphasis falls on comparative statics of the subject under investigation, and the human reference is minimised. Besides, there is an implicit, sometimes explicit, assent to the view that large-scale changes like these, though composed to a considerable extent of many instances of human activity, cannot be the product of human purposes and must be largely unanticipated and unintended. The leaders of the *tiers état* in the National Assembly could not have foreseen the Terror or Napoleon, let alone the rise of nationalism, industrialisation and bourgeois hegemony in France and beyond, all of which could be traced back to the impetus given by the Revolution.[14] The most prescient of nineteenth century British administrators and governors hardly foresaw the birth of Pakistan, the trend towards socialism in India and the survival of caste despite much transformation.[15] And the original Orthodox Jewish leaders of an obscure Judaic sect of Christians before AD 70 could hardly have envisaged the effect of Paul's message and their own demise in the Jewish rebellion.[16]

Functionalist analysis is largely the study of this mode of intransitive change, being concerned with functions or 'objective consequences' of collective patterns of activity. Functionalist analysis as distinct from functionalist theory, may be utilised as much for the study of unanticipated and unintended changes, as for the more usual study of pattern maintenance and stability. That is, if one accepts the strict distinction between active and passive modes of change.

But change may be the outcome of human plans and inten

24

ions. Voluntarist change of this sort accords with the transitive meaning of change in sentences like 'he amended the constitution', 'Muhammad altered the course of history', 'the Nazis destroyed the German class structure', 'the Chinese communist commune provides a model for agricultural development in the Third World', 'Courbet and the Realists revolutionised artistic subject matter and treatment', where each refers to intended changes, either effected or, in the Chinese example, in process. To confine oneself to this sort of change is to focus on the role of individuals, movements and groups in the analysis of pattern alterations and event sequences. It is not just human activity which becomes central, but conscious, willed and planned activity, even the act of choice itself.

The transitive usage of the verb 'to change', carries a dramatic connotation. An active relationship between the subject effecting change and the object undergoing it is implied in such cases as a regime implementing reforms in local government or taxation, synods adopting a new liturgy and ritual, or businessmen introducing new sales policies. Even where the object is a property or aspect of the subject, in phrases like 'he changed his position (in the argument)' or 'Beethoven changed his style in 1803', there is the same dramatic, evential quality. This sense of change implies a break with past patterns of behaviour or beliefs, and a conscious dynamic movement to another pattern.

For the study of micro-events the active mode of change is obviously more apposite than the passive. But what of processes and trends of change? Can they too be analysed in terms of this active and transitive mode? If not, ought we to discount and ignore all statements of change that cannot be translated into transitive, human terms? For, clearly, many processual changes can be so translated: conquests, colonisation, urbanisation, migration, unionisation, revolution, social movements, cultural innovation, trade relations, sect formation, carry strong connotations of planned, conscious human

25

activity, even where the results fall some way short of any
one of the initial blueprints. But there are other medium-
duration changes, not to mention trends, which appear to
elude such active formulations; to recast the process of alleged *embourgeoisement* of the working class in terms of conscious human action appears contrived and seems to miss the
point. No doubt, the translation could be effected by analysing the clash of different values and the dilemmas of privatised
workers in operational terms, as the Luton survey did; but
this already admits a degree of social constraint emanating
from long-term trends unamenable to short-range change,
which sets limits to the element of human agency in effecting
changes. The human choices derive from the preceding
changes in opportunities and situations.[17]

The active mode of change appears even less relevant for
long-term trends. Of course, the decline and fall of the
Roman Empire was the result of a confluence of human
actions on the part of individuals and groups pulling in
different directions and proposing alternative solutions to the
immediate problems. Different emperors, generals and barbarian chiefs canvassed various plans and made successive
choices; yet by no stretch of the imagination can we attribute
Rome's fall to a conscious decision and plan, as we might
Persia's at the hands of Alexander.[18] When we come to geosocial changes, the role of human choice and action is almost
whittled away, as man or earlier species try to ward off the
perils of the environment. Only with the Magdalenians, do we
trace glimpses of alternative conceptions and choices in the
cave sites chosen and painted, and the bone implements
utilised.[19]

The longer the time-span taken, the less important become
individual or group choices and plans. Moreover, the further
back in time we reach, the smaller the role of rational human
activity. Once again, we must beware of allowing the peculiar
circumstances of the present era to inflate our picture of the
role of human action in change. Nor do I think we are debar-

red from analysing long-term trends, unless they can be re-
duced to (or retranslated into the terms of) human choices.
Such a strict human eventialism would be arbitrary and
barren, given the paucity of records of earlier periods.

On the other hand, a full as opposed to schematic analysis
of processes and trends will attempt to tie its account to such
chronological event sequences as the records reveal; and since
many event sequences refer to human actions, there is a
strong practical case for their use as ultimate referents.[20] In
other words, a more complete picture of trend changes would
incorporate as many references to sequences of human
choices as records permit without loss of too much perspective. In practice, it is always a question of balancing the
demands of comprehensive coverage with concrete depth.

Beyond these practical considerations lies a moral commitment to understanding the role of human choice in history.
It is ultimately this value position which justifies the tracing
of connections between group and individual decisions in the
processes and trends of change. This is all the more relevant
when the emphasis falls on the 'social' component of historical change. Since human interaction is governed to some
extent by norms and ideals of conduct, modifications and
replacements of the patterns of human association, triggered
by sequences of human choices, must form the core of any
adequate analysis of historical change viewed as *social* change.
Herein lies the significance of Weber's canon of 'adequacy of
meaning', of taking into account at the very heart of the
analysis the moral views and conceptions of the participants
in any chain of events. In dealing with long-term trends, such
understanding may be impossible; but it is never unnecessary
or secondary, except perhaps in the very earliest periods.

Such a commitment explains the attention given to social
movements and cultural innovation in this book, and the
selection of models and theories which illuminate the problem of the relation between non-human event-sequences and
successions of human choices in effecting processes and

27

trends of change. I shall examine theories which minimise the role of human agency, as well as those which allow it more scope; but it is particularly with their treatment of the *relation* of active and passive modes of change that I shall be most concerned.

3 Images of change

Images, metaphors and analogies abound in all social thought, but nowhere more pervasively than in our thinking about social change. In fact, most models and theories of social change derive from one of two archetypal images, each of which contain variant metaphors and analogies. Sometimes, theories may attempt to combine elements from both families of images, to produce a grand synthesis or cope with a refractory problem, but generally the emphasis of a given perspective upon social change is weighted in the direction of one or other of the two basic 'families' of images. It is possible and fruitful to trace the formulations of these theories, however abstract and remote they appear, to their underlying imagery, and this chapter relates the two basic frameworks of social change in the nineteenth century, namely social evolution and classical diffusion, to their metaphoric substrata.

Continuity and 'flow'

Undoubtedly the most potent and dominant images in Western thought are those which picture change as a relatively smooth, continuous and ceaseless process, a homogeneous flow of social patterns and units in time. To some extent, flow imagery takes a single aspect of change, and the most tangible, namely motion itself, as in Heraclitus' ever-renewed river of time, and lets the precondition stand symbolically for the process of change, highlighting the ceaselessness of change rather than its evential quality or its novelty. Only in the idea of expansion as events pile up in history can the river metaphor begin to convey the simplest notion of pattern modification, an extension of scale. More complex images of continuity and flow assume some development of patterns and units, in addition to mere expansion. A very popular source of imagery is mountaineering. The course of civilisation, knowledge or technology may be likened to the ascent of a slope, represented most simply by a straight line, or by a logistic curve in the case of population growth, or even an exponential curve (compound interest) where technical inventions are concerned.[1] As these examples show, ascent images take the largest entities as their subject; population, science, religion or civilisation throughout history. These are also the entities with which the still fashionable step and stage models of ascending rungs or plateaux of change concern themselves. Here continuity and flow are definitely interrupted. Modernisation theories like Lerner's threefold stages of tradition, transition and modernity, fall into this category.[2] So does Lenski's updated series of techno-economic stages, ranging from simple hunting and gathering societies, through horticultural and then agricultural, to modern industrial societies.[3] Alternatively, one finds one or two big 'steps' or 'humps' like the Neolithic revolution and industrialisation dividing long intervening periods resembling plateaux of stability.[4] Common to all ascent versions is the assumption that later stages or plateaux mark a considerable advance in knowledge, technology and social opportunity over earlier more restricted ones.

Cyclical theories form another set of flow images of continuous change, in this case with a marked emphasis upon the repetition of the seasons or the ebb and flow of the tide, or man's daily, weekly or yearly round. Cycles often carry organic metaphors, particularly in the rise-and-fall of empires or civilisations; sometimes a mechanical analogy is preferred. Pareto's circulation, or rather alternation, of elites is a case in point. Pareto sees societies as in a state of dynamic equilibrium; movement by any part will cause automatic readjustments in the position of the other parts. Changes in the psychological make-up of ruling elites will therefore automatically be compensated by corresponding changes in that of the subject non-elite. A ruling elite requires a judicious blend of two sets of psychological qualities, those of bravery, aggression and force characteristic of the 'lions', or in late nineteenth century Italy the conservative rentiers; and those of the 'foxes', the entrepreneurs and speculators who are cunning, flexible and adaptable. The cycle begins when the qualities of the foxes swamp those of the lions among members of the ruling elite. Fraud replaces force, and the elite become unfit for rule. If they cannot cream off the compensating psychological elements from the leadership of the non-elite in time, they will be ousted by a counter-elite emerging from the ranks of their subjects who possess in abundance the required qualities of force and aggression. The new elite in time becomes subject to the same inevitable process of dilution of its qualities or 'residues', and the cycle then begins again.[5]

Repetition and cumulation are essential characteristics of a third set of continuity images, namely those of organic growth, and especially that of the life-cycle in all natural species. The metaphor echoes the Psalmist's pessimism: 'As for man, his days are as grass. As a flower of the field, so he flourisheth. For the wind passeth over it and it is gone, and the place thereof shall know it no more',[6] and Homer's realistic resignation: 'As is the life of the leaves, so is that of man. The wind scatters the leaves to the ground; the vigorous forest puts forth others, and they grow in the spring-season. Soon one generation of men comes and another ceases'.[7]

Such imagery of plant growth and withering, and such metaphors of the seasons, served Spengler in his classification of the eight ideal cultural wholes and their phases of archaism, maturity and decay. All his units, which are really cultural

31

styles, traverse identical phases in their life-cycle; but it is doubtful whether Spengler was really as interested in the aspect of *Untergang* as in the correct delineation of a culture's essential stylistic qualities.[8] There are no such doubts with Danilevsky's scheme of twelve 'culture historical types', each of which possesses its own basic plan, which it will realise in the course of its life-cycle. As a biologist, he uses the language of the organic analogy freely; one of his themes is that the period of efflorescence is short compared to those of development and decay.[9] Finally, Toynbee's massive *Study of History* examines the rise and fall of twenty-one civilisations, most of which traverse his stages of genesis, growth, breakdown and disintegration. Some, it is true, are arrested growths or deviant types, but their status derives from the application of the life-cycle analogy. In this Toynbee remains in the Gibbonian tradition, as also in his emphasis on moral qualities of the societies whose course he charts.[10]

Growth and social evolution

Nisbet argues that the life-cycle image is the dominant metaphor of social change in Western thought. But in fact it is not the life-cycle idea itself which has proved so attractive, but the elements of potentiality and immanent development underlying it. The most influential theories of social change extrapolate from the first half of the life-cycle, that of genesis and maturation, and go on to assert this condition of all patterns and units taken as a single series. It is not so much the growth and decay of particular units which has exercised such fascination in the thought of the last two centuries, as the idea of unlimited progress of mankind or civilisation or society throughout history.[11]

The essential metaphor behind such evolutionist thinking is that of society as a plant or animal, possessing an intrinsic capacity for self-development and growth. Change is located in this inner potential for self-realisation, and is equated quite simply with the process of unfolding that potential. Change is like the flowering of the seed; external conditions may facilitate or impede growth, as do soil and climate; but they form only a background for change, not part of its mechanisms. Those mechanisms and processes lie within the unit or pattern under consideration, and may be discerned in the relationship already existing in embryonic form in their most rudimentary stages. When, for example, Durkheim undertook to study the social function of religion, he justified his choice of the primitive totemism of the Australian Arunta by explaining that sociologists must return to a structure's simplest and most primitive form, so as to show 'how it developed and became complicated little by little', until it became the fully developed set of patterns which constitute religion today.[1][2] Similarly, Rostow's analysis of the take-off into economic growth sees change as essentially a function of relations and mechanisms within the society under investigation, viewed as a fairly isolated, self-propelling entity. Of course, growth may be arrested, as it can be in organisms; but, if successful, its course is prescribed and continuous through all the stages to that of mass 'high consumption'.[1][3]

The organic analogy is often taken as the point of departure for the various schemes of social development proposed by the classical evolutionists of the nineteenth century. In fact, the notion of developmental stages antedated by at least a century its biological underpinning, particularly in its Darwinian form. It can already be discerned in the quarrel of the Ancients and the Moderns in the late seventeenth century, and even Spencer, who is often thought to have applied organic concepts to social life, arrived at his developmental theory before Darwin's publication of the *Origin of Species*. Besides, as has often been noted, Darwin was concerned with mutations between different species, whereas the social evolutionists were interested in the processes of change within a single species, man. Similarly the entities of which such stages of development were predicated were large-scale units like civilisation, religion or culture, viewed as a single, if differentiated, process throughout history.[14]

There were, of course, considerable differences between the various social and cultural evolutionists, as regards the chosen entity of study, the actual stages demarcated, and of course the particular examples selected for each stage. For present purposes it is the common elements which underlie their schemes, which are important. What interests us here is the extent to which evolutionary perspectives, indeed any theories which derive from basic metaphors of continity, flow and growth, can account for historical changes and for the role of human action in change.

The first common element in classical evolutionary schemes is their holism. Society, culture, the family, religion, knowledge, civilisation, are viewed as unities, whose parts are interdependent. These unities or wholes alone form the subject of any analysis of change, since they are more than the sum of their parts. Change is not change of any part or of its relationship with other parts, but only progress of the whole. Examples are Spencer's differentiated and integrated societies, Durkheim's types of social organisation, Marx's modes of production, Westermarck's forms of marriage, or Morgan's 'states of civilisation'.

Second, change of these wholes is continuous and cumulative. That is, it would be possible to show that for the whole course of a given pattern or unit–institution, society or civilisation–viewed as a single historical entity, change in that unit was gradual, relatively smooth and involved no radical discontinuities or intrusions. The series of stages which could be distinguished were products of an orderly succession, a lawlike development, in which the preceding stage accumulated elements until a point was reached in which their density gave rise to a new, higher stage of that unit.[15]

Of course, this assumption did not pertain to the particular examples of the entity. A specific religion, family system or society might experience all sorts of convulsions, intrusions and conflicts. Societies and civilisations might founder and perish, but the type remained until it gave rise through its own development to its successor stage.

Third, change resulted from the operation of forces and mechanisms within the pattern or unit. It is at this point that evolutionism came closest to the basic premise of the organic analogy, even where it did not subscribe to the idea of the life-cycle or adopt Darwinian notions. Religion, society and civilisation contained within themselves the capacity of self-development, for unfolding the potential lying within: that explained the naturalness and ubiquity of change. Change constituted a basic propensity or 'law' of every pattern or unit, because the latter possessed a developmental capacity and a need for self-realisation.[16]

Fourth, evolutionary schemes generally posited a uniform direction of change from simple to complex forms, and from the homogeneous to the heterogeneous. They also assumed an increase in the size of units, or an extension of their range. This constitutes a fundamental thesis in Spencer's sociology. Aggregation of the parts through a process of individual reproduction coupled with unions between small groups, is accompanied by specialisation of functions within a more highly organised and larger unit. In the *First Principles*, Spencer wrote:

> The advance from the simple to the complex, through a process of successive differentiations, is seen alike in the earliest changes of the universe to which we can reason our way back, and in the earliest changes which we can inductively establish; it is seen in the geologic and climatic evolution of the earth, and of every single organism on its surface; it is seen in the evolution of humanity, whether contemplated in the single individual, or in the aggregation of races; it is seen in the evolution of society, in respect alike of its political, its religious and its economical organisation; and it is seen in the evolution of all those endless concrete and abstract products of human activity, which constitute the environment of our daily life. From the remotest past which science can fathom, up to the novelties of yesterday, an essential trait of evolution has been the transformation of the homogeneous into the heterogeneous.[17]

As a result, Spencer obtains a classification of societies into simple, compound, doubly compound and trebly compound, a typology not unlike Durkheim's combinations of simple hordes into simple and doubly compounded polysegmental societies.[18] Similarly, Morgan's series of the development of civilisation from the state of savagery to barbarism and finally civilisation carried with it implications of increasing cultural and institutional complexity. As he put it:

> As it is undeniable that portions of the human family have existed in a state of savagery, other portions in a state of barbarism, and still other portions in a state of civilisation, it seems equally so that these three distinct conditions are connected with each other in a natural as well as necessary sequence of progress.[19]

A fifth common assumption was really a corollary of the idea of a uniform sequence and direction of change. All the evolutionist schemes made a strongly ethnocentric use of the comparative method to back their claims, and in particular treated England and France as the exemplars of modern civilisation and progress, and contemporary primitive peoples as representatives of the earliest, most rudimentary stages of human history. Speaking of these primitive societies, J.F. McLennan wrote:

> Their condition, as it may today be observed, is truly the most ancient condition of man. It is the lowest and simplest and in the science of history old means not old in chronology but old in structure. That is the most ancient which lies nearest the beginning of human progress considered as a development.[20]

Tyler, too, looked back in this respect to the 'conjectural history' of the Scottish Enlightenment historians, in particular to Ferguson, when he declared:

> The institutions of man are as distinctly stratified as the earth on which he lives. They succeed each other in series substantially uniform over the globe, independent of what seem comparatively superficial differences of race and language, but shaped by similar human nature acting through successively changed conditions in savage, barbaric and civilised life.[21]

In the present context, the important point about the use of the comparative method is that it provides a means of establishing a hierarchy of societies, institutions or civilisations, which is spatial and temporal as well as logical. The fundamental criterion of the series is an equation between modernity, as revealed in Western societies, and maturity; conversely, traditionalism suggests immaturity and lack of development. All the evolutionary schemes were really only elaborations of this fundamental contrast or polar continuum. And, together with the assumption of immanent potentiality, serial comparison constituted the essential background of explanations of social change offered by classical evolutionists and their modern descendants.

I say 'background of explanations' advisedly, because some of the evolutionists were careful to add that their serial comparisons afforded, as Tyler put it, 'but a guide, not a full explanation'.[2 2] Comte, too, was quite aware of the 'extremely unequal degree of development' attained by different populations for reasons which are 'little understood'.[2 3] Nor have I insisted on a feature commonly attributed to classical evolutionists, namely, an over-determinist unilinear developmentalism. Spencer was explicit on this point. Although a broadly cumulative development from the simple to the complex and differentiated may be discerned in the history of human society taken as a single entity or idea, actual societies are full of differences; indeed 'there have arisen genera and species of societies' as the result of both different histories and differing environments; so that 'like other kinds of progress, social progress is not linear, but divergent and redivergent'.[2 4]

Similarly, not all evolutionists were wedded to the idea that the causes of change are always the same, beneath the accidents and local particularisms of historical cases. True, all evolutionists searched for an encompassing formula for various types of change; and the formula tended to be conceived of as a rather rigid framework, even a 'law' of development,

37

be it economic or intellectual or more strictly social.[2][5] But most evolutionists were also ready to admit other causes of change, not only of specific historical changes, but also of whole classes of change, such as the transition from Spencer's 'militant' societies to his industrial ones. The fact is that the evolutionists were not particularly interested in mechanisms of change from one stage in the series to another; for, if change was an immanent process to that which undergoes it, if it was in fact a realisation of what lay within the unit, then what need to look further for additional causes of change? At best, the latter would be contributory, at worst mere catalysts.

I have dwelt at some length on what I think is the common framework of assumptions behind classical evolutionism, because it forms the essential background for an understanding of modern 'neo-evolutionism' whose contribution to our problem of historical change, its sources, channels and effects, is assessed in the next chaper. As will by now be clear, the common framework of classical evolutionism is largely irrelevant for the analysis of the event-produced pattern substitutions which define social change. This is not meant as a criticism, since evolutionists did not view their task as concerned with the explanation of historical changes.[2][6] Their interest lay in the delineation of a logical-temporal series or hierarchy of types of a given, abstracted entity like religion, the family, society or civilisation. Their real contribution lies in the classification of social and cultural difference, in what was called social morphology, not in the search for generalisations about sources, channels and effects of actual changes in specific institutions or cultures. At the same time, their assumptions and approach, and the underlying image of cumulative flow which they encapsulate, remains a potent force in the work of many recent theorists who *are* concerned exactly with our problem of historical changes, and their explanation. Before considering these theories, however, I want to look briefly at the other major archetypal image of change in Western thought, and its typical nineteenth century offshoot.

Intrusion and 'rupture'

In recent years images of history and social change which stress radical discontinuities have become popular again. In some ways, this represents a reaction to the alleged failure of neo-evolutionism. It also derives from concern with relations between the advanced industrial and the developing countries, and with the possibilities and impact of revolutionary social movements.

On the other hand, the underlying images behind recent discontinuity theories are as ancient, if not quite so pervasive, as the 'flow' metaphors of evolutionism. Break, rupture, collision, impact, intrusion, penetration, cleavage and revolution are just some of the terms for the notion of a fundamental transformation and replacement of patterns and units, or between two states of the same unit. The origin of such images is closely bound up with a longlived popular attitude to life as the plaything of chance, epitomised in the ancient Roman worship of Fortuna. Even today many historians, concerned with the rich detail of cultures and political institutions, the myriad permutations of international diplomacy and war, or the impact of 'great men', still insist on chance as against historical inevitability, and on the uniqueness of once-for-all events. Particularly at the micro-event level and in the political region, where human action is vital, chance and the role of random events are invoked with greater frequency.

But it is not only chance events which upset the stable order and well-laid plan. Social institutions and groups are continually subject to the clash of 'forces', originating either within or outside the pattern or unit. The metaphor of collision of social forces draws attention to basic incompatibilities in the elements composing units, an inability either to separate or to readjust to each other. Such is the case with interest groups or self-interested economic man in Marxist and utilitarian economics respectively; the struggle of value ideas emanating from incompatible world views which Weber analysed; the tensions of 'races' and ethnic groups described by sociologists from Gumplowicz and Park to Banton and van den Berghe; Dahrendorf's coercion theory of latent conflict between organisational powerholders and their subordinates; and the clash of interests between exploiting centres and regional peripheries with which both Gunder Frank and Shils, in different ways, have been concerned.[28]

Still more systematic images of discontinuity appear in works which revolve around the idea of radical breaks or 'rupture' in the very fabric of social patterns and units. Examples are the opposition and gulf between basic paradigms in various sciences, the analysis of social revolutions, and the destructive impact of intruding cultures. To see history as shaped largely by periodic, boundary-breaking intrusions of event sequences or patterns, which create an upheaval in the established order and a radical gulf between it and everything that follows, is to undermine the very possibility of a cumulative and uniformitarian sequence of historical stages. The play of chance, the collision of forces, may, after all, be dovetailed with a flow metaphor, an image of history as continuous process; but, to posit incommensurate ruptures and gulfs in patterns and units, regarded as the result of differential intrusion and impact, is to deny the possibility of silent growth or flow beneath the accidents of history.

Strict rupture metaphors imply a horizontal view of history. What comes after the break may or may not be more advanced or progressive than the pre-existent patterns; it matters little, in any case, in comparison with the fact of upheaval and rupture as the cause of change, and of intrusion from outside the pattern or unit as the cause of upheaval. The interest of such images, and their derived theories is focused, not on a comparison of pre- and post-rupture states as a 'step-theory' might be, but on the causes and channels of the rupture itself. Time, too, is divided into a number of bounded periods, the punctuations being created by intrusion or collision of patterns emanating from disparate units. A consequence of this horizontal, non-serial, view, is the emphasis on spatial properties, on a wide field of crosscultural, continental, even global phenomena held to be either interacting or potentially so; and also a much greater stress on the impact of, and relations between, the unit and its environment.

It is for theories derived from this kind of image of change that Martins has recently coined the term 'caesurial.'[29] The growth in appeal of caesurial theories surely reflects our experience of the rapidity of changes today, and a feeling of bombardment by events, processes and trends emanating from a wide geographical and sociological spectrum. The result is a sense of an absence of relationship between increasingly shorter periods in the life of individuals and groups, and of the contingency, multiplicity and permutations of causal chains which intersect. The problem then becomes one of making sense, of ordering, such an array of apparently contingent chains, a problem discussed in later chapters.

Invaders, elites and culture contact

A rather different offshoot of intrusion and rupture images is represented by the varieties of diffusionism, especially those which flourished at the turn of the century. Here it is important to distinguish classical diffusionism of the early twentieth century from recent revivals of diffusion and culture contact at the micro-event or process levels. Classical diffusionism represented at the outset both a critique of evolutionism and an attempt to construct an alternative framework for the explanation of historical changes, particularly at the trend and process levels. In other words, it was concerned with large spatial categories (societies, civilisations) and with both long-term and medium-term periodisation. Here I confine my remarks to classical diffusionism and consider the revival of micro-diffusion in chapter 5.

Classical diffusionism is sometimes labelled 'hyper-diffusionism' by those later diffusion-oriented anthropologists and archaeologists like Boas and Childe who remained interested in processes of diffusion as part explanations of various states of a unit or pattern, but rejected diffusionism's claim to provide a total framework, or its attempt to explain particular changes wholly in terms of one or more conquests or migrations. In hyperdiffusionist explanations, the impetus of change was *always* assumed to be external to the unit or pattern underlying it. Similarly, change was always contingent, since processes and events which impinged on the unit were historically random and always traumatic. This was especially true of the popular invasionist and elitist varieties of hyperdiffusionism.[30]

Invasionism dominated prehistoric archaeology till the Second World War. Whereas evolutionary approaches tended to explain the successive strata of cultural assemblages on the great prehistoric sites in terms of internal development, of a gradual and almost imperceptible movement to the next, higher stage, the 'invasionists' looked to the sudden intrusion into an area of a new culture and hence new tribes, and their imposition by force of arms of their more advanced culture and its artefacts on the existing inhabitants. It was implictly assumed that the invaders' culture and technology was more advanced than those of their victims; and further that lower cultures could advance only to a very limited extent by their own unaided efforts. To break through to a new cultural phase, to change the existing patterns altogether, required the intrusion, often bloody, of tribes bearing a different culture. For example, the transition from Mousterian to Upper Palaeolithic blade cultures in Western Europe some 40,000 years ago or more, was explained in terms of invasions and an influx of tribes from the culturally more advanced Middle East.[31] Similarly, Childe's later explanation of the advent of Neolithic farming in Europe attributed it largely to the spread of men, ideas and techniques across southern Europe from the earliest centres of grain production and animal domestication in Iraq and Palestine.[32] This accorded well with the ancient historian's traditional concern with military conquest and ethnic migrations, starting with the founding of the al-Ubaid culture in Sumer by migrants and continuing with Sargon of Akkad's military unification of Mesopotamia right up and across to the Roman conquest of Gaul and Britain and the barbarian irruptions after Constantine.

Of even greater, though more shortlived, popularity was the elitist hyperdiffusionism of Eliot Smith, Perry and Raglan.[33] Here, too, the Middle East figured as the source of cultural change. Eliot Smith, for example, proposed the idea that primitive peoples owed whatever advancement in civilisation they manifested to the peaceful labours of a missionary elite (the 'children of the sun') from Egypt. Only Egypt (for Raglan it was Sumer) possessed a favourable combination of geography and social circumstances, a unique accident of nature, since man was essentially uninventive and needed the stimulus of either a unique constellation of circumstances or of the example and precept of more advanced peoples. Hence, outside the favoured centre(s), civilisation could only result from a diffusion of waves of missionising elites, bent on bringing the benefits of culture to their less fortunate brethren. One consequence of this was that the farther removed from a centre a given area was, the more diluted its forms of civilisation tended to be. Another was that distant areas were likely to manifest over time more 'decadent' survivals of that civilising impulse.[34]

Despite the absurdities of such single-culture reconstructions of history, these schemes do offer valuable correctives, particularly to the notion of developmental stages whether for every society or for the whole of humanity. The most important was that migration and demonstration effects (i.e. the movement of men and ideas) were constantly altering existing patterns and units. Even if we cannot go as far as the theory of culture circles proposed by Frobenius, Graebner and Father Schmidt in reconstructing world history on the basis of random cultural connections through intermittent similarities in the traits of remote cultures, we are more ready to accept the role of cultural borrowing, as a result of our experience of modernisation and ethnic contacts.[3 5] 'Stimulus diffusion', the diffusion of central ideas, still plays an important role in our thinking about the development of civilisations and social structures.

4 Neo-evolutionism

Since the Second World War there has been a revival of evolutionary thought in both cultural anthropology and functionalist sociology. The attempt to marry functionalism with some of the evolutionary presuppositions marks the most influential of those theories and frameworks which draw their inspiration from underlying images of flow and continuity. 'Neo-evolutionism', as this theoretical framework may be termed, shares with classical evolutionism its basic aim of comprehending in one account the processes of social order and social change, which will show both the orderliness of change and the innate tendency of every order to undergo change. On the other hand, modern neo-evolutionism departs from its predecessors in two important respects: first, in emphasising medium-sized entities such as isolated cultures and societies as the subjects of analysis in respect of change processes, in addition to the largest and most abstract entities of civilisation or humanity throughout history, and second, in making serious attempts to explain the causes and mechanisms of changes, in addition to classifying the forms change takes at different periods of history. It is this historical intention we must examine, to see how far a framework derived from assumptions we saw to be largely irrelevant for the study of historical changes can succeed in coping with the problems and issues raised by the diversity of concrete changes.

Social Change

Multilinear evolution

As one might expect, neo-evolutionism, a derivative of organic approaches, is best suited to the task of explaining longeval trends, especially in the realm of culture. Here two issues present themselves: the first, that of isolating an overall direction of change in history for the largest entities, and of relating that trend to the specific instances of changes; the second, to explain the sources and channels or mechanisms by which change takes place in both the largest and in the medium-sized entities, that is in humanity, civilisation, religion and society, and in particular cultures, societies, religions, or sequences of them.

The distinction between these two issues, and between the two levels of entity, forms the point of departure of an influential attempt by Sahlins and Service to rescue evolutionism from the limbo into which it had been consigned after the First World War.[1] They argue that we can discern an overall trend in human history, a progressive movement, which they describe in terms of the criterion of evolution proposed by Leslie White, namely, the total amount of energy production and transformation in a society. White had shown that there had been an evolution in the largest entity, humanity over the whole of history, in the direction of increased utilisation of energy resources and greater mastery of man over nature.[2] Even if it is conceded that White's criterion of overall or 'general' evolution is rather too narrow and technological (though he does go on to relate it to other cultural variables), there is indeed something to be said for classifying societies and cultures in terms of a quantitative criterion, so long as we do not mistake such a series for a covert explanation of change, either in the largest or in medium-sized entities.

In contrast to the 'general' evolution of humanity, Sahlins and Service sharply distinguish the 'specific' evolution of particular segments of humanity, namely the particular cultures and societies into which men have been historically divided.

Here Sahlins and Service draw on the work of Julian Steward
on cultural variation. Steward's form of evolutionism is often
called 'partial' or 'multilinear', since he was concerned only
with the development of particular cultures in their ecological settings. These cultures were viewed as discrete entities,
each of which faced peculiar problems of adaptation to its
environment. It was, in fact, through increased adaptation to
its environment that a given culture assumed its distinctive
form; and the wide variety of ecological niches explained,
according to Steward, the increase of cultural variation over
time. While at the beginning of history, cultures in different
areas might develop along similar lines because of a rough
similarity in their ecological settings, as time went on cultures
became more specialised, and hence more variegated, because
of changes in their environment to which they were forced to
adapt.[3]

Now, according to Sahlins and Service, the difference
between these two forms of evolution, the general and the
specific, may amount in particular instances to outright conflict. Specific evolution implies increasing adjustment to an
environment, general evolution increasing autonomy from
and mastery over an environment. Specific evolution may
actually lead to what Geertz termed 'involution', a counter-
evolutionary trend; the society or culture may become so
adapted through specialisation to its environment, so well
adjusted in its ecological niche, that it is no longer *adaptable*,
no longer able to innovate for a leap forward to higher levels
of technological and social organisation. Geertz's example is
the early twentieth-century Javanese economy, which became
so embedded in its 'late Gothic' agricultural and social setting,
so ornate, intricate and complex in its social and economic
arrangements, that continuing ecological pressure of population in a labour intensive rice economy simply created an
impasse and hindered all innovation for increased productivity
or better technology.[4] So that rather than increased specialisation leading automatically to higher stages of evolution, as

some classical evolutionists thought, intense adaptation through specialisation may actually hinder development and lead to social dissolution or stagnation.

To a large extent the discussion of long-term directions in human history amounts to little more than a rough classification of societies in terms of quantitative variables like the increase in knowledge, technology and population. As such it has only a very general bearing on the more specific trends, processes and micro-events of historical change. A given level of knowledge or population sets limits to, or allows a range of possibilities for, change. It neither originates that change, nor provides its channels, nor dictates the forms which change will take. Hence, the main kind of evolution with which we are concerned, is that termed 'specific'; and the only thesis to emerge here is Steward's hypothesis of ecological adaptation.

Apart from the charge of a teleological bias, the central difficulty of such an ecological hypothesis as an explanation of mechanisms and forms of cultural change is the greater variability of cultural forms over physical environments. In simple hunting and gathering societies, indeed, which possess a rudimentary technology, men are so dependent on their environment that we are entitled to look for the sources and channels of cultural change in the first place in the peculiarities of their physical environment. But beyond this level man's increasing control of his environment, his growing capacity for transforming it, makes it increasingly unlikely that such sources and channels will be found only in the physical environment. The environment tends to set limits to cultural variation and change, rather than propel the unit towards change. Besides, with highly complex changes like those that initiated the irrigation civilisations of the Nile, Tigris and Indus, important mental as well as physical factors were at work. Coulborn, for example, argues that the cults of Osiris and Enki in Egypt and Sumer were concerned with water control, and were coeval with the first settlements at Abydos and later Memphis, and at Eridu and al-Ubaid, set up by the new immigrant tribes.[5] Along with population pressure, soil exhaustion and progressive desiccation of surrounding areas, the new religious cults and the 'mental exaltation' they engendered were essential for coping with ecological dangers and furnishing migrants with hope of survival and security in their new settlements. From a slightly more diffusionist standpoint, Daniel points also to the stimulus provided by ideas taken from neighbours or trading partners, especially in the rise of the civilisations of Egypt and the Indus.[6] Finally, the cyclical theorists also emphasised a certain parity between ideational and material factors, especially in the definition of a civilisation's distinctive style.[7]

The lack of correlation between cultural forms and changes, and physical environments, appears even greater as we move forward in time. Once civilisations have established themselves the relative autonomy of religion and art, for example, is greatly enhanced. One has only to think of the tenacity of Islam or Buddhism or Christianity in a variety of physical and social settings, especially as regards their theology. Similarly, the major artistic languages, such as the Western tradition of pictorial space, have spread from Greece and Italy (with gaps and intervals) to a wide range of physical habitats and social structures; and more important, the changes to which those languages and traditions have been subjected bear no relation to changes in the environment. The same is true of linguistic or legal changes, especially in more recent history. Cultural changes appear to owe more to external contact with other cultures, and to changes in stratification and political control, than to environmental pressures.[8]

Cultural differentiation

A more sophisticated attempt to account for the diversity of cultural changes in large units in neo-evolutionary terms is to be found in the recent works of some functionalist sociologists. Their central thesis is that such change is largely the result of internal differentiation of a pattern or unit at a given point in time. By a process of differentiation they mean much more than the economists' division of labour or specialisation of tasks, more also than Durkheim's complementarity of roles producing a measure of social harmony.[9] They view a given structure or process as a system of mutually dependent parts, each of which fulfils its function for the maintenance of the system. Systems are in perpetual motion, a state of dynamic equilibrium in which the parts or roles are continually readjusting to each other and to changes in the subsystems of which they form parts. Hence a system always contains a drive towards achieving new states, a disposition to change. Significant change, however, requires more than a readjustment of a system's roles; it requires the generation of new sets of roles, each of which is more specialised than its predecessor, and hence more adaptable and better adapted. It also requires a reintegration of the new role-sets in a more effective unit. Significant change is therefore structural, and the differentiation that produces it is also structural: for it alters the general and constraining pattern of relationships between the existing parts of a system in a manner that endows the unit with greater effectiveness in relation to its environment.[10]

How do the functionalists employ their notions of structural differentiation, reintegration and greater adaptability to account for cultural change? The answer is that 'differentiation' is made to perform two separate tasks, first the delineation of structural types or, if you prefer, of the forms change takes; and second, the explanation of the process of change to a new type, or of the sources and channels of change.

As regards the first, it is the degree to which systems of symbols, norms and codes are differentiated which determines their position in the evolutionary series. Bellah,[11] for example, in his studies of religion, posits a process of increasing differentiation of their symbols, practices and organisation. Historically, he argues, it is possible to discern 'stable crystallisations' of interactions in symbols, practices and organisation at each level of complexity. Five such levels of crystallisation present themselves: the primitive, the archaic (Egypt and Mesopotamia), the historic (Weber's 'world historic religions'), the early modern (early Protestantism and ideologies of developing nations) and modern (the West today). Bellah then traces a process of growing dualism in religion as differentiation increases. Primitive religions are barely differentiated, and no distinction is made between the self and the world. Archaic religion, and even more historic religion, sharply oppose self and the world, as religion itself becomes separated from the rest of society. This dualist trend ends in complete otherworldliness, which lasts nearly two thousand years from *c*.500 BC to the Reformation, when a this-worldly trend sets in, which is optimistic and change-oriented. The final phase of differentiation is apparent today only in the West, where individual achievement and personal reinterpretation of religious symbols and practices have become the main religious criteria: in Jefferson's phrase, each man has become a sect.

A slightly different use of cultural differentiation as a classificatory criterion is that of Parsons in his well-known *Societies, Evolutionary and Comparative Perspectives*, [12] where it is the growing specialisation of the cultural system and its autonomy *vis-à-vis* the social system, which distinguishes levels of social evolution. Here again, we have a basic threefold division of history (civilisation throughout history) into primitive, intermediate and modern stages; but since the middle category is broad enough to include every empire and civilisation from Egypt and Sumer to the Renaissance, Parsons subdivides it into 'archaic' and 'advanced' intermediate. The specific criterion employed is the degree to which writing, as the key to the differentiation of culture from society, has become diffused to those outside a small coterie of priests and scribes. A second criterion is equally cultural: the degree to which an archaic cosmology has become universal and philosphical, a development which Parsons believes only occurs when priestly organisations no longer have a monopoly of literacy.

As an evolutionary scheme, Parsons's is neither simply unilinear nor multilinear in Steward's sense. For though he acknowledges that some societies which did not develop into more advanced types found adequate social 'niches', and other societies like ancient Greece and Israel were able to originate new cultural developments though they themselves failed to survive independently, he can only envisage a single main stem of evolutionary advance, namely the 'Western' from Israel and Greece through Rome to the modern West. All the rest, it is clear, have proved evolutionary failures, however well adapted to their environment they may be. Such a cladogenetic scheme is plainly ethnocentric. Its series is derived from a selective reading of Western history, in terms of attributes which have proved significant and valuable in the social experience of industrial Western states, notably America.[13]

Do such hierarchical series help us to explain the forms that change characteristically took in the civilisations or religions which experienced it? And does the differentiation principle serve a useful classificatory function? To both questions, the answer must be largely negative. The concept of differentiation yields a continuum of finely graded distinctions rather than a series of clear cut-off points, or stages. Its historical applications are also less than clearcut and useful: within religion some aspects may be differentiated, like Indian philosophical thought in Hinduism, while others like caste activities may remain tightly ascriptive. A universal religion like Islam may display little differentiation of religious and political roles, particularly under the Caliphate, and its belief in an inscrutable God (i.e. otherworldly dualism), was quite compatible with a strong this-worldly and optimistic faith in God's world.[14]

The utility of a classification based on the autonomy of culture is also rather limited. Parsons cites ancient Judea as a 'seedbed' society, that is, a society whose culture could be hived off, as it were, from its social structure, to initiate further cultural developments in other societies which adopted, and adapted, some of its elements. Yet surely few societies were so closely meshed with their religious culture as ancient Judea.[15] In this respect at any rate Roman law provides a better example of relative autonomy. But even here, it is not the social-cultural dichotomy as such which is important, but the fact that societies like Judea and Rome, which differ very greatly in their degree of complexity, can equally provide sources for the diffusion of some of their traits.

I do not for a moment wish to deny that structural differentiation has not occurred in many societies, or that the division of roles and institutions into more specialised subsystems does not have important consequences for the whole unit. A given level of differentiation is certainly one of the important factors in conditioning the reception and forms of the *next* set of changes. The difficulty lies in attempting to make this factor the sole basis for a taxonomy of societies which is simultaneously a logical series in a scale of adaptability. A further difficulty arises in the attempt to square the differentiation series with a chronological progression. Parsons is certainly aware of these difficulties. He tries, for example, to show how societies and civilisations may be graded, not merely in terms of their structural differentiation, but according to the distance they evince from purely ascriptive and particularist bases. In other words, he supplements the differentiation criterion with tests drawn from his 'pattern-variables'.[16] But that, in effect, merely compounds the difficulty of providing a clearcut logical classification which is also a temporal series. We must conclude, then, that differentiation, like achievement and universalism, describes one of the forms taken by change, but that it is neither invariable, nor basic to the diversity of such changes. So slender and residual a taxonomic base can hardly serve to order the rich diversity of cultural changes.

Tradition to modernity

Matters are hardly improved when we turn to the second of the two tasks for which functional neo-evolutionists employ the term 'structural differentiation', namely, that of explanation of the sources and channels of change. The difficulties are well illustrated in the case of a transition which is a favourite with neo-evolutionists, the emergence of modernity, first in Europe and then in Asia and Africa. Again, this is a type of change most suited to growth images, since it involves longeval trends which are economic as well as cultural; but it also requires recourse to a lower level, the intermediate timespans of processes, a fact welcomed by those functionalists who intend an explanation of historical change in comparative terms.

As will emerge, there are considerable differences of emphasis and approach among neo-evolutionists in their treatment of the problem of modernity. At the most general level, that of human civilisation as a whole, or of its major institutions, a reversion to Spencerian ethnocentrism is marked. Because of the historical fact that it was in certain Atlantic seaboard states that men first learnt to apply inanimate sources of energy to production and thus to maximise control over their environment, so the main features of those states and their cultural and social organisation have become normative, not just for classifying other societies in terms of approximation to the West, but for supplying the main elements of an explanation of the emergence of the peculiar complex of modernity.[17] So, because, for example, legal codes and institutions occupy a vital position in modern Western societies, and because they exemplify vividly the formal rationality of procedure which Weber noted, they become for Parsons the main area in which differentiation of culture from society generates the transition to modernity, both in the West and outside.[18] Parsons sees law as a cybernetic control system for regulating the higher energy yields of modern Western society. Similarly, Bellah locates the source and channel of modernisation in the rise of flexible capacity to learn from experience, which is the result of increasing differentiation of organisations and roles.[19] And yet, when he goes on to examine Asian responses to the Western impact, Bellah is perfectly aware that a variety of responses like nationalism, cultural reform or neotraditionalism may, and have, served to induce maturation and modernism. The Protestant ethic in Europe has many analogues outside.[20]

Underlying these explanations of the transition to modernity is the assumption that specialisation of roles and institutions and their reintegration on a higher adaptive level constitutes an advance of the rationalisation process. Differentiation inevitably breeds rationalisation. Rationalisation in turn is both precondition and central feature of modernity. Parsons even interprets Weber's studies in the sociology of religion, and the latter's more general essays on the subject, in evolutionary terms. Parsons understands Weber's central contrast of magical and rationalised attitudes and conduct in terms of 'regressive' and 'progressive' evolutionary tendencies. Whereas Weber recognised a direction of change within one civilisation, namely rationalisation in the Occident, Parsons equates the latter with the pattern variables of achievement, universalism and functional specificity, and then uses it to measure and account for the evolution of civilisation as a whole. Again, Weber does not trace a process of structural differentiation in the societies or religions he studies; when he alludes to such differentiation, it is not as a cause of change or even a classification of structures, but simply as a condition of further changes.[21] Finally, Weber rarely employs Parsons's principle of dichotomous differentiations, or alternative directions of the historical process, which either reinforce or attack the existing order. But such an oppositional method, which underlies the pattern-variables, is a necessary device of every systemic approach which operates with a framework of immanent change; whereas an antiholist like Weber who, as we shall see, has no use for immanentism, is not committed to a dichotomous conception of change processes.[22]

I have cited Parsons's interpretation of Weber's *Religions-soziologie*, not only to bring out the contrast between his very generalised neo-evolutionism, so far removed from specific historical processes, and Weber's more particularised historical sociology, but also because Weber's *Protestant Ethic* thesis has provided an essential element in other neo-evolutionist approaches to the rise of modernity. Of these, the most historically relevant and comprehensive is Eisenstadt's account of the emergence of European modernity. Modernity is viewed as a great tradition, based on the assumption of expanding rationality, of the 'possibility of the active creation by man of a new sociopolitical order, an order based on premises of universalism and equality'.[23] This assumption first developed in Europe, and owed much to its various traditions, city-state, Imperial and feudal, but perhaps even more to the development of commerce and secularism from the fifteenth century. In the consequent restructuring of European society, the Protestant Reformation played a crucial role. Eisenstadt argues that, after they failed to realise their original goal of a total religious transformation of society, the Protestant movement were able to transform their own religious impulses by revolutionising society. They did this by fostering new kinds of roles, especially that of the entrepreneur, which accorded with the economic ethic of Protestantism, and new types of institution, for example, states and laws based on ideas of a covenant or contract between parties or between rulers and ruled. In the Catholic countries, on the other hand, the Counter-Reformation stifled tendencies towards greater social and political diversity and new ideas about statecraft, culture or economic activity. Economic roles, in particular, could not gain autonomy from states and municipalities; in Luethy's formulation, Catholic 'finance' was tied to a given political order, while 'Protestant Banks' were relatively autonomous.[24]

The key to Eisenstadt's analysis is the concept of transformative capacity or potential. Every tradition and belief system contains within itself antithetical religious and value orientations. In the Protestant faith, several elements are uneasily combined: transcendental predestination, this-worldliness, individual activism, unmediated relations between the individual and the sacred. Eisenstadt does not say whether it is the content of any or all of these tenets, or their tension in combination, which endows Protestantism with its transformative potential. From his earlier analysis of tradition, however, we may gather that it is the latter possibility, which is more decisive.[25] The direction in which Protestant transformation led was a greater autonomy of the political, cultural and economic spheres from each other:

> The specific transformative potentials of Protestantism can be seen in the fact that it took up these seeds of autonomy and pluralism and helped in recrystallising them on a higher level of differentiation than in the Catholic countries, like Spain and France, where the potentially pluralistic impact of various modern trends, including Protestantism, was inhibited by the formation of the Catholic state during the Counter-Reformation.[26]

But again we are not told exactly how this was achieved. Eisenstadt rightly emphasises an aspect neglected by Weber, namely, Protestantism's role in transforming the 'central political symbols, identities and institutions', especially in providing legitimation for new types of authority relations and in forging new symbols of national identity; but he does not indicate how Protestantism actually affected politics or how its 'possibilities' were translated into action, except to mention Luethy's political thesis which sees in the return to the Bible, coupled with the situation of religious wars, new bases for legitimating authority and forging identities.[27]

From the foregoing the reader will realise that Eisenstadt's

analysis is much more closely related to actual historica
trends and processes than those of other neo-evolutionists
but that it still operates within a theoretical framework o
structural differentiation. This is especially true of Eisenstadt'
account of how the new directions initiated by Protestan
transformation came to be institutionalised. Just as a highe
level of differentiation is the end result of the process, so i
differentiation a precondition of absorbing new goals. Once
again, a single theoretical criterion determines our perceptior
of European modernisation, and Dutch, English and Scandi
navian developments are judged to be more decisive than the
experience of France or Italy. Because the northern countries
were already, apparently, more open and pluralistic, they
could more easily absorb a 'world-changing movement' like
Protestantism by transforming their own institutions.

But even if we limit our discussion to the conditions of the
ideological rationale of modernity in Europe, that is to
'modernism', it becomes impossible to select one of the many
causal chains involved in the genesis of so complex a phenom
enon, at the expense of the others. Neo-evolutionists follow
Weber in concentrating on the effects of the Reformation fo
the growth of tolerance and ascetic capitalism. But equally im
portant were the impact of Renaissance humanism and state
craft, or the expansion of European horizons and trade ini
tiated by Italy, Spain and Portugal.[2 8] Nor can we overlook
the revolutionary impact of the Roman revival and the com
parisons with antiquity which shook France in the century
from the quarrel of the Ancients and Moderns through the
Enlightment to the Revolution.[29] The countries men
tioned were, of course, much less affected (if at all) by Protest
antism and its transformations. Yet France especially contri
buted some of the abiding traits of modernism (including its
zest for revolutions); and since the sixteenth century Europe
as a whole has experienced more than one purifying and
transformative movement.

Neo-evolutionists are equally selective in their treatment of on-Western modernisation. Levy,[30] for example, contrasts he structures of 'relatively modernised' with 'relatively non-modernised' societies in terms of the familiar functionalist ariables, of specialisation, self-sufficiency of subunits, or heir integration, achievement, universalism and centralisation. Ie defines modernisation as the use of inanimate sources of ower over animate ones, and of tools to multiply effort. But when he turns to the impact of modernisation from more advanced societies, he sees it largely in terms of introducing rganisational specialisation and 'compartmentalised thinking'.[30] The channels and forms of modernising change remain argely processes of differentiation, integration and increasing ationality.

This is not to say that neo-evolutionists do not distinguish he exogenous route of non-Western modernisation with its ndigenous development in Europe. Eisenstadt certainly insists upon the contrast.[31] At the same time, this vital contrast f route does not occupy the centre of neo-evolutionist concern with modernisation. Whether the source of modernisation is internal or external to a unit is much less important han its mode of response to any stimuli, and its direction. Apter, for example, thinks that non-Western modernisation differs from Western versions in sequence rather than in causes or direction. In the West commercialisation bred industrialism, which in turn led to modernity and thence to advanced industrial societies. Outside the West, commerce coupled with bureaucracy brought modernisation, which generates industrialism. Apart from the role of bureaucracy, the overall process of modernisation is similar both within and outside the West, and this is because Apter adopts a broad, all-encompassing definition of modernisation as the movement to increasing rationality, flexibly differentiated structures and a social system that maintains itself through constant innovation.[32] Similarly, Almond's classification of 'agrarian' and 'industrian' societies is based on the pattern-variables of ascription versus achievement, diffuseness versus specialisation and particularism versus universalism, and so is the general trend from the first to the second type.[33] Again, the interest of neo-evolutionism is largely confined to a system's response to external or internal forces, a response which is viewed as inherent in the nature and state of that system. In this vein, Eisenstadt argues that China was poorly adapted to meet the Western challenge of modernity, because the close links between her political, social and cultural orders inhibited the development of reformist or transformatory tendencies. Her Imperial centre, Confucian ideology and ruling *literati* were too closely interdependent to allow a constructive, adaptive response to the Western impact. That is why both emperors and Kuomintang could only retreat into a defensive 'neotraditionalism', which tried to uphold strong central institutions and a unifying ideology. It required an appeal to the reformist traditions of some *literati* and gentry, and the rebellious traditions of peasantry and secret societies, to enable the Communists to found a new strong centralised order. And they only achieved their goal, Eisenstadt indicates, by adopting a Western, Marxist-Leninist ideology and by fighting a war of national liberation against the invading Japanese.[34]

Despite his acknowledgement of the complexity of historical sequences and the impact of external factors, Eisenstadt shares the general neo-evolutionist interest in the overall trend of structural differentiation revealed by the process of modernisation. The transition from tradition to modernity is identified with a universal movement from simple to complex, and is also caused by it. This overworking of the concept of differentiation leaves important questions unanswered. Why, firstly, does differentiation figure as the prime determinant of change? And why, secondly, do only some structures have the capacity for self-differentiation? And how, thirdly, is this trend related to the processes and events which play so large a role in actual historical changes?

Disturbance and strain

Further light on these questions, and particularly the last, is thrown by the neo-evolutionist treatment of medium- and short-term processes and events in the political sector. For, more recently, neo-evolutionists have turned to a consideration of many issues which their classical forefathers relegated or neglected: social movements, political revolution, race and ethnicity, and war.

From the political angle the transition to modernity has been fraught with strain and disturbance. These concepts are central in neo-evolutionary analysis of contemporary change. But they also illuminate the overall role of differentiation in the neo-evolutionary framework. In discussing the strains of modernisation, both Smelser and Eisenstadt single out the protests and disturbances generated by the growing structural complexity which accompanies economic development. Smelser, in particular, has traced the roots of all kinds of mass movements and outbursts to a failure of the social system to maintain order in change. The rapidity of modernisation is particularly liable to produce 'lags and bottlenecks' and 'severe discontinuities'.[35] Yet strain and malintegration are symptoms of all kinds of social change. This is because differentiation is a universal and fairly continuous process. Structures are always becoming more specialised, their parts increasingly growing unlike each other. Groups, norms and institutions are always becoming more diversified, and so there is more likelihood of conflict over goals and resources. Hence the parts of a system are always in danger of becoming poorly integrated, of producing tensions and clashes. Conversely, the more strains and tensions in a society, the more heterogeneous in values and interests does that society become: and the more heterogeneous, the greater the likelihood of individual specialisation. And so on, until we reach a state of atomisation and dissolution; or until the strains produce such a state of anomie that people panic and suc-

cumb to some religious or ideological movement which pro
mises a better life through social unity.

This same general argument underlies Smelser's study of
the strains accompanying the Industrial Revolution, as in his
analysis of modernisation processes and of 'collective out
bursts and collective movements'. In dealing with the change
over from farming and domestic production in England to
large-scale factory industries, Smelser traces a seven-stage
sequence of disturbance and innovation. His starting-point
is an example of strain: dissatisfaction by weavers who adopted
Kay's loom and by entrepreneurs with the performance of the
spinners.[36] This dissatisfaction spilled over into hostility and
violence, and the police and courts proved unable to control
worker 'disturbance'. Only thereafter were new ideas brought
in, reforms drawn up and incorporated in new institutions like
business firms and trade unions. In the same way 'strain' is
the mother of modernisation. For economic development
and differentiation are accompanied by strains which in turn
produce anxiety and disturbances. Only when the old social
controls prove ineffective can new agencies of reintegration
at a more specialised level become acceptable, and so reduce
the fears and protests of men and women whose lives have
been dislocated by rapid change.[37]

This emphasis on strain and dissatisfaction as initiators of
change in Smelser's scheme, casts some light on why differentiation is singled out as the prime determinant of change. For
neo-evolutionary analysis consists in an uneasy combination
of equilibrium models and assumptions of immanent growth.
Even if the equilibrium model is conceived in dynamic terms
as a continual process of readjustment among moving components, there remains a considerable tension between these
two rather different images of change (even if they belong to
the same metaphoric family); and this tension is reflected in
concepts like 'strain' and 'malintegration', which evoke both
the idea of growth pains and the notion of mechanical breakdown, which could only result from continual differentiation.

By the same token, however, neither strain nor its parent differentiation can help with our second problem: why some structures can become differentiated while others cannot. For, according to the assumption of immanent growth, every structure possesses this capacity, whereas history quite clearly contradicts the notion of equivalent capacities. Neo-evolutionists tend to be pragmatic about this dilemma. Structures which have in fact become differentiated, they argue, possess the capacity, while the rest are incapable of differentiation from within, and it becomes necessary to appeal to some external source of change to overcome the deficiency, as was the case with Eisenstadt's example of modern China.[38]

But it is with regard to the third question, the relation of differentiation to historical processes and events, that the weakness of neo-evolutionary schemes is most apparent. The very breadth and generality of their categories of explanation and description makes it possible to apply them in so many different contexts that their explanatory edge is blunted when it comes to dealing with more specific historical sequences. In the analysis of social movements and revolutions, concepts like Smelser's 'structural strain' and 'generalised belief', which form key links in his 'value-added' methodology, are more useful as terms in a logical hierarchy than as elements in a temporal series, let alone an explanatory scheme. They serve to organise the varied array of historical materials into serviceable descriptive categories, but fail to provide any explanatory mechanisms.

We can grasp this failure better by considering these categories and their relations in more detail. Smelser argues that the major social movements and political revolutions are examples of 'value-oriented movements'. That is, they aim to reconstitute the basic values of society, not just some specific institutions or norms. By changing these values they *ipso facto* revolutionise its social structure. Now such movements only arise in societies which are 'structurally conducive' for such movements, that is, where men define their situations entirely in value-oriented terms and are politically disinherited, where they seem to have no alternative means for reforming their position and their grievances receive no recognition. Here one can think of various outcast or subject peoples, both in medieval Europe and the overseas colonies. The specification also appears to fit the position of both peasants and bourgeoisie in eighteenth century France, and of the workers in late nineteenth century Russia. Similarly, with Smelser's next category, 'structural strain'. Under this heading he places the various ambiguities, discrepancies, deprivations and conflicts which afflict men in these situations. It is again a very broad category, since there is hardly a stratum or group or even a role which is not subject to some sort of strain. Certainly, the peasants, workers, bourgeoisie and outcasts or colonised experienced a variety of deprivations, tensions, ambiguities and the like.[39]

Smelser would accept this stricture. His real contribution to the analysis of mass movements rests on the role of his next category, the emergence of a 'generalised belief', which gives meaning to and explains the situation for the disinherited. Smelser sees in such beliefs a means of reducing the ambiguities of a situation which is felt to be insupportable. The believer has come to feel that his social world is evil and must be purged. An ideology appears to offer an escape and an explanation of the menace. Ideologies are elaborate examples of generalised beliefs, which include hysteria, wishfulfilment and hostility, and always involve a 'jump from extremely high levels of generality to specific, concrete situations'. This is what Smelser calls 'short-circuiting', a total, all-embracing belief, in contrast to an empirical, piecemeal realism. Now such ideologies serve as cures for strain, they explain the situation, they unite a host of grievances under a single, potent myth. Here Smelser is thinking of the scapegoat myths of millennial movements like the Franciscan Spirituals which attacked the Pope as Anti-Christ, or of the Nazi myth of Aryan superiority.[40]

It is only when a generalised belief has taken root that the other stages in the value-added process come into play. These are precipitating factors like the harvest failures of 1788 and 1789, or the Great War and bread riots in St Petersburg in 1917; mobilisation of the participants for action, often through the activities of charismatic leaders; and finally the absence or ineffectiveness of social controls both before and during the collective movement.[41]

There are a number of difficulties in this analysis. To begin with, the categories as indicated are too broad for comfort. It is difficult in practice to know in which category to classify a particular process. Why should we regard the lot of medieval peasants and artisans, or non-whites in the colonies, as examples of 'conduciveness' rather than 'strain'? What is the criterion for inclusion here? Second, can we really place complex ideologies like nationalism and communism on a par with simple expressions of hostility and anxiety as 'generalised beliefs', and regard both simply as short cuts and cures for deprivation and strain? Is this not an example of psychological reduction, which completely neglects the cultural meaning and content of different beliefs? Moreover, why do similar strain situations give rise to such varied beliefs? Third, the categories embody a rather negative view of social movements and revolutions as basically unable to affect the fundamental value patterns of a society. But Smelser's pessimism stems from the extremely general way in which he defines the terms 'values' and 'central values' of a system. But, with one or two exceptions, even the most general of values have undergone modification, be it in our valuations of man, of the deity, of sex or material possessions, or of the ends of life, and revolutions and social movements have played an important role in initiating or consolidating such changes.[42]

Beyond these difficulties, there remains the central problem of historical explanation. Can a scheme such as Smelser's help to explain mass movements like communism or nationalism, or revolutions like the French or Chinese? Can we really derive the genesis of ideologies and movements from conditions of strain? Is the role of human agency in the shape of charismatic leadership and absence of social controls, so dependent on unseen and unplanned structural situations?

The same problem haunts Johnson's theory of revolution. There too it is the structural conditions—disequilibration of the system, dysfunctions in the division of labour and in values, loss of authority, strain, and 'accelerators' of revolution—which produce a revolutionary situation, while the actions of men in power or outside, are treated as important but secondary causes.[43] While Johnson, like Smelser, concedes that the outbreak and success of revolution depend on chance factors or 'precipitants', and on the skills of ruling elites in controlling the situation, he treats these factors as secondary and dependent in the growth of a revolutionary situation.[44] Both Smelser and Johnson tend to infer the inevitability of such situations from the occurrence of a revolution. They then trace its sources in the multiplying social strains and maladjusted personalities within that system. When a system's roles and values no longer harmonise, when its institutions and norms appear ambiguous and contradictory in their demands on individuals, the latter can no longer adjust and adapt to such dislocating circumstances. Over a longer period, they become disoriented and maladjusted, full of anxiety and hostility. It is in this state that men become obsessive revolutionaries and join mass movements like nationalism, fascism or communism. Like Kornhauser, who locates the revolutionary tinder in the unattached crowds of urban conglomerations, the neo-evolutionist sees the perceptions and actions of men as epiphenomena, mere mechanical adjuncts, of social stress. The question of individual choice and variable perception hardly arises in these over-determined schemes of forces and factors.[45]

Growth and change

Whether we are confronted by questions of cultural change, economic modernisation or political movements, neo-evolutionary accounts reveal a fundamental and systematic failure to come to grips with actual historical processes of change. Their schemes and categories can be applied to so many sequences of events, their concepts are so lacking in precision, that their utility and meaning is diminished the nearer we approach the world of specific changes. As classifications of change, neo-evolutionary categories like differentiation and reintegration remain too vague and partial to provide a systematic taxonomy, except perhaps at the level of 'general evolution', in which case we are dealing with a purely logical hierarchy, which must not be confused with a temporal series or read back into trendlike sequences of actual change. As explanations of change, concepts like transformative potential or strain or maladjustment are so broad in their application, and so all-encompassing, that they may deflect attention from the task of research into actual sequences of events and their causes. Moreover, they automatically curtail the area of human agency to a marginal footnote. Man's understanding of his situation, his evaluation of his dilemmas, becomes unidimensional, a mechanical reflection of situational imperatives whi h overwhelm him. It is only when neo-evolutionists depart from their framework and formulae and analyse the range of responses to new situations that they concede a larger role for certain groups or individuals in realising changes. This is especially true of Eisenstadt's incorporation of elite analysis into his account of modernisation.[46] Eisenstadt sees these elites as mediating the Western impact, and more generally as controlling the processes of differentiation and the resultant crises. For modernisation brings inevitably demands for participation in central decision-making by groups which had previously been silent or ignored. Indeed, modernity may even be defined in terms of the cap-

67

acity of the 'centre' to absorb such demands and incorporate into its machinery the participation of new groups who clamour for adequate representation. Only modernising elites can institutionalise the new goals and values through organisations able to regulate conflict, like schools, unions, courts, welfare agencies, the state itself. And the actual route to modernity will depend upon the type and orientation of the society's elite at the time.[47]

Yet this very example encapsulates the central dilemma of neo-evolutionary accounts of historical change. The more the neo-evolutionist incorporates factors derived from a study of the actual processes of change, factors like elites, class conflict, protest movements, in short collective human agency and will, the less relevant and necessary becomes their neo-evolutionary scaffolding of differentiation, reintegration and adaptation, and the less can we discern overall evolutionary trends in historical change. The central weakness of their accounts is an overdetermination of changes, which is a function of the retrospective neo-evolutionary reading of a Western history treated as normative, or of the 'spirit' of modernism which has allegedly brought evolutionary success to the West. The second major weakness, which stems from the first, is an explanatory failure. So concerned are neo-evolutionists with the direction and forms of change that they tend to subsume the results of change under categories so broad that it is an easy step to treating them as causes and channels of change as well. This is what has happened with their key concept of differentiation. The result is to divert attention away from the other two essential elements in any theory of change, namely its sources and channels, in favour of the third component, the forms or repercussions of change.

Both weaknesses, overdeterminism and explanatory inadequacy, spring from the same source, an assumption, even an insistence on, the immanence of change to the unit undergoing it. Change is viewed as growth, interrupted perhaps, but always reaching forward and upwards away from the simple and rigid to the complex and flexible. But, as we shall see, only certain kinds of change follow this pattern, mainly quantitative indices of mobilisation and modernisation.[48] Cumulative changes interact with the more 'caesurial' kinds of change associated with historical processes and events; and even the long-term trends favoured by neo-evolutionists, are often composed, not just of cumulations of knowledge or technology, but of discontinuous historical processes and events, in ways that we have only begun to study. In these processes and events a large role must be assigned to human volition, particularly collective agencies, even where the results, as so often, do not correspond to human intentions.[49]

Beyond this, there remains the salient fact, so often overlooked by neo-evolutionists, that much change results from the impact of processes and events external to the unit undergoing it; and that, in certain circumstances, the state of that unit is less important than the nature and channels of external impact.[50] Other peoples' decisions, made without reference to a given society or group, and even in far-off units, may affect the members of that society more than all the strains and maladjustments and potentialities within their own society, just as the decisions and plans and conflicts of that society may have unforeseen consequences for their neighbours or for more remote units. It is not only non-Western units who suffer intruding events and processes. The West itself (and in previous ages all civilisations) has become what it is today because of a continual pattern of interrelationships with neighbours and more distant units. Similarly, the distinctive institutions and groups within the West, or the 'third world', are today what they are, more because of the impact of other neighbouring institutions and groups, than as a result of some unseen, innate potentiality, which only the neo-evolutionist can discern beneath the accidents of history.

5 Diffusion

A large part of social change consists in the institution of novelties. Innovation and its channels are the main foci of interest for all kinds of diffusionist studies, from acculturation and communications theory to research into adoption of inventions, marginality and the role of social comparisons and movements. 'Channels' and 'mechanisms' of change constitute the intermediate component of any theory of specific changes, between, as it were, the sources of origins and the repercussions and forms of the change. Diffusionists though differing on many points, are united in their belief that changes originate mainly outside a given unit or pattern, and that the researcher's duty is to locate the peculiar, if recurrent, channels through which a change exerts its influence on a particular unit or area.

The return to diffusion

Diffusionism, as we saw, has a considerable ancestry. Already in the nineteenth century, Tarde had drawn attention to the role of social imitation in establishing habits and attitudes, and in the early twentieth century Thomas and Znaniecki analysed the acculturation of immigrant ethnic groups over generations, and their status as emigrants from Poland and immigrants to the United States.[1] Similarly Park in the 1920s advanced the idea of 'location' in his studies of urbanisation. He argued that ethnic and population movements into cities could be best analysed in terms of the concept of geographical

70

and social space possessing its own structures and statuses and containing regular patterns of movement. Social and cultural products of such movements he divided into a cycle of phases such as contact, competition and conflict, leading later to acceptance of new migrants through mechanisms of accommodation.[2]

After the Second World War interest in processes of diffusion began gradually to revive. The reasons for this revival are instructive. The war itself, and its offspring the United Nations, emphasised global interdependence and patterns of conflict and alliance. Even more important, the rise of many new states in Asia and Africa, stimulated interest in processes of aid and development of poorer countries. The arrival of ethnic groups in the West, and the vast increase in travel abroad, also turned sociologists' attention to questions of race and culture contact. So did the revolutions in communications. Radio, television, cinema, computers, satellites, all of which may precede modernisation in poorer countries, nourished a completely different approach to the study of social change in terms of networks of communications.[3] So, more indirectly, did growing bureaucratic encroachments on privacy, and the use of electronic surveillance, which redirected attention to novel methods of control and access to units and patterns. More recently still, the rise of international networks of revolutionary movements, guerrilla or terrorist, ranging from the Japanese Red Army and the Weathermen to the IRA, the Angry Brigade and the Baader-Meinhof group, have impressed on observers the impact of often violent events and processes in the life of even the most peaceful and well-ordered societies.[4] In a more profound way, historians and sociologists have been forced to revise their traditional adherence to the fundamental categories of 'nations' and 'societies' by the many international links and unions between 'anticolonialist' movements and elites; and to recognise the role of deviant groups as carriers of change. Similarly, the subtleties of the international status order, and changes in relations between power and economic blocs, have re-emphasised the international and interstate context of 'development' and even of internal social structures.[5]

There have also been intellectual reasons for the return to a study of diffusion processes. The most obvious of these is dissatisfaction with sociological models which, particularly in mid-century America, emphasised synchronic relations and static patterns. Of course, the same dissatisfaction has bred the expansion of mainly functionalist interests in the direction of formulating the neo-evolutionist theories discussed in the last chapter. But for a number of reasons many scholars felt unable to accept these frameworks, which still operated within the confines of the nation-state as the terminal sociological unit, both for theory formulation and data collection. This limitation was powerfully reinforced by strong, if latent, national sentiments and the practical advantages offered for data collection by government social surveys.[6] In view of the various transnational and international links described above, diffusionists have felt such neo-evolutionist models as unnecessarily restrictive.

From a diffusionist standpoint, there are even more serious objections to neo-evolutionism than this methodological limitation. The most important objections were:

1. a failure to grasp the cardinal role of external influences on a unit, whether these influences were borrowed or imposed;
2. an underestimation of the influence exerted by the channels of diffusion on the forms of change;[7]
3. a marked tendency for neo-evolutionism to substitute serial classification for explanatory hypotheses involving empirical processes;
4. the equation of events with mere accidents or stimuli impinging uniformly upon the growth properties of periodically 'malintegrated' social systems;
5. the minimisation of the role of human choice and perceptions in the introduction and diffusion of novelty.

All diffusionists would subscribe, by definition, to the positions entailed by the first three objections, and most tend to emphasise 'events' and 'human choice'. They vary, however, in their understanding of the role of both, and in the relative proportions of each in the genesis, diffusion and institutionalisation of change, a point to which I shall return shortly.

Recent diffusion theories have two reference points. The first is classical diffusionism. Recent diffusion theories adhere to the basic premises of earlier diffusionism, especially its exogenous model, its empiricism and eventialism. They differ, however, in aims and scope. Classical diffusionism was allembracing; its aim was to reconstruct the course of human civilisation and 'explain history'. Recent theories make no such claims. Instead they focus on selected empirical processes and aim to show their relevance and importance for an understanding of *some* types of change. That is why I have chosen to refer to recent models as 'diffusion theories' rather than 'diffusionism': 'micro-diffusionism' also catches this shift in emphasis and scope to the smaller-scale, shorterspan sequences.

As we shall see, not all recent models are so limited and modest in their ambitions, and in these cases we are faced with a much broader exogenism, which subsumes every kind of diffusion process without singling out any particular ones. But by far the greater number of recent models have a micro-diffusionist emphasis; and that is partly because they arise through a dialogue with neo-evolutionism or functionalism Neo-evolutionism, therefore, constitutes the second reference point of most recent diffusion theories, just as classical evolutionism constituted the reference point for classical diffusionism. Recent diffusion theories vary, however, in the closeness of their ties with neo-evolutionism, and this allows us to classify them according to their degree of proximity to neo-evolutionism and functionalism.[8]

Communications

Undoubtedly the most influential type of diffusion theory

has been the 'communications' analysis of Ithiel de Sola Pool, Pye, Lerner and especially Karl Deutsch. In the early 1950s, they began intensive research into the impact of the mass media in transmitting messages both on an interpersonal and a collective level. In this respect Deutsch's work on social mobilisation was especially fruitful. Deutsch argued that societies are composed of clusters of networks of individuals connected by an intensive division of labour and transport facilities. Cultures, however, are defined by information networks: a 'people' or ethnic group may be described as 'a larger group of persons linked by such complementary habits and facilities of communication', or more simply, 'wide complementarity of social communication'.[9] The process of national or cultural assimilation which creates new cultures or extends old ones is often accelerated by the drive of urbanisation and migration which mobilises people for more intensive communication. It is true that cultural and social assimilation can proceed without such mobilisation, though it may take several generations; Deutsch cites the slow conversion of the Copts to Arabic in Egypt, and the seven hundred years of gradual extinction of the Cornish and Wendish languages.[10] Generally, men who have been uprooted from their local surroundings and become a public receptive to many sources of information are readier to forsake old habits and memories for the standardised culture of the cities to which they are exposed, or, where there is conflict between culturally different groups in the cities, to accentuate it to the point of demands for secession. The rate of change, whatever the direction, depends largely on the economic and technological drives to migration and urbanisation, which are then filtered through the collective learning processes of different social groups.[11]

A similar model of social mobilisation and assimilation underlies Daniel Lerner's influential theory of modernisation, in his *The Passing of Traditional Society*.[12] The same transnational phenomena, modernisation and nationalism, which had inspired Deutsch's work on research and research methods, were now incorporated into a systematic framework revolving around two key variables: psychic mobility and the mass media. On the whole, Deutsch was more interested in the structural and sociodemographic factors affecting perception and individual consciousness. This comes out particularly clearly in the indicators he uses to measure the rate of social mobilisation in Finland, Bohemia, India and Pakistan and Scotland. They include urbanisation, employment in secondary or tertiary industries, conscription, taxation, schooling, literacy, mass media exposure, trade flows and voting. Lerner takes over this kind of correlation analysis and quantitative approach in his investigations of Middle Eastern modernisation, but he places greater emphasis on the development of certain types of personality and individual receptivity. Moreover, his theory of the transitional society and personality located between the restrictive traditional and open participant modern types of society and personality, is a good deal more determinist and ethnocentric. It is also more impregnated with imagery drawn from the mass media and more conscious of the effects of the channels of communication themselves, as opposed to the content of the messages.

Lerner starts from the same point as Deutsch: physical and social mobility, especially urbanisation. Thereafter he emphasises two (in his view, closely linked) variables: literacy and exposure to the mass media. He then claims that 'the media spread psychic mobility most efficiently among peoples who have in some measure achieved the antecedent conditions of geographic and social mobility'.[1][3] With the final indicator of modernisation, namely political participation as manifested in voting, these variables form a determinate sequence of stages of development. The dynamic features of his model are, however, psychological. The mass media function as an interior 'mobility multiplier'. Cinema and television bring the opinions of mankind to bear on the individual and allow him to imagine himself in a whole range of situations, creating a world of vicarious experience. They teach a man 'interior manipulation', enlarging his identity. That is the secret of empathy, the 'capacity to see oneself in the other fellow's situation', and empathy or a mobile sensibility is the main precondition of efficient operation in a changing world.[14] In other words, modernisation derives from innovation and innovation from the new kind of personality which desires change. Modern Western societies are populated by empathic personalities; unfortunately, the transitional societies of the Middle East are filled with discontented souls, ambivalently admiring Western values and institutions, but rejecting Western domination. Such men, like the Grocer of Balgat whom Lerner takes as his type case of 'transitionals' in Turkey and elsewhere, have begun to empathise, to imagine themselves in new roles, but remain bound to their traditional situation with its narrow horizons. The overall result is a frenetic and extreme nationalism.[14]

Despite considerable differences of emphasis, Deutsch and Lerner share a broad interest in the conditions of economic development and modernisation, and more generally in 'processes' of change, as opposed to trends and micro-events. Not that they neglect the latter completely. Lerner, in particular, is concerned with the micro-events of interpersonal attitudes and capacities. Such events are not the unique intrusions with which historians have been most concerned: they are classes or sequences of collective and repetitive events, namely, the transmission of messages between members of traditional rural societies or underlying populations. Or they are units of behaviour in response to these messages—migration to the city or other lands in the hope of betterment, or xenophobic nationalist demands stemming from ambivalence and insecurity. Or the events may be elements of a process of political socialisation, in which men and women whose traditional societies have been dislocated by external change try to discover a new social and political identity, and so become capable of building up adaptable organisations. Thus Pye claims that 'the story of the diffusion of world cultures has been one of countless efforts to establish modern organisational forms in traditional, status-oriented societies'.[16] It is 'citizens in transitional societies', especially those in power, who are most disturbed by 'the consequences of cultural diffusion'.[17] In this way Pye and other political scientists studying change in the new states of Africa and Asia have attempted to relate broader exogenous processes of diffusion to the small-scale changes associated with interpersonal relations and political socialisation.[18] Making use of Eriksen's concept of a crisis of identity, particularly in the charismatic leader, who expresses the collective search for a national idenity, Pye, Verba and Almond have attempted to relate the processes of cultural communication in a polity (i.e. the political culture) to the typical make-up of its constituent personalities and to the disturbances they suffer in periods of rapid change.[19] In this way, a communications approach to political change can make use of the abundant data on political recruitment, political interests and practices, and the influence of political values and sentiments on the course of events.

Of particular interest, from our standpoint, is the manner in which different communications approaches can be harmonised with a systemic outlook or with neo-evolutionary frameworks. To begin with there is often a common interest between the two approaches: to produce a theory of orderly growth and even a recipe for surmounting instabilities. Both subscribe to a view of the progression to modernity based on Western experience. Both admit deviations and disturbances along the route, but regard these as temporary. Even more important, both approaches view the whole process of modernisation as the major example of a much more general historical trend towards complexity, flexibility and a widening of social participation. Deutsch, it is true, has also emphasised the increasing self-sufficiency and self-preoccupation of nations today, a trend which may impede their flexibility. But even this prognostication is founded on an almost neo-evolutionist stress on the increasing complexity of society and government, where more and more groups have to be satisfied.[20]

The fact is that 'communication', in the special sense of the term as used by these theorists, is part of the process of social learning; and social learning in turn comes very close to Bellah's insistence on maturation and Eisenstadt's pre-occupation with societies which can absorb change while retaining their basic features intact. It is in this fundamental sense that a 'communications' theory, far from being opposed to neo-evolutionism, actually reinforces it by pointing to some neglected empirical processes of assimilation and social learning. This also largely accounts for the acceptance by this kind of diffusion theory of a larger neo-evolutionist framework in dealing with longeval trends as opposed to micro-events. It is only at the latter level, and in Deutsch's case at the intermediate process level, that such 'theories' are original. In other words, 'communications theory' turns out to be a species of 'diffusion without diffusionism', or 'neo-evolutionism with diffusion'.

Marginal man

Lest this last formulation sound too paradoxical, we should recall that as early as 1865 Tyler had asserted that 'civilisation was a plant much more often propagated than developed', and that classical evolutionists were quite aware of the often complementary role of processes of external diffusion and indigenous development.[21] The insertion, therefore, of diffusion processes into a more overarching neo-evolutionist framework, should hardly surprise us.

Indeed, quite often we encounter models which attempt to harmonise the two approaches. One of the best-known accounts of empirical processes of diffusion, Everett Roger's *The Diffusion of Innovations*, which collates research findings on innovation in such fields as technology, agriculture and medicine, employs a systems framework to order the results of this collation. Innovation, he contends, occurs within a situation, which is best viewed as a social system. The end of all action is interpersonal security, a 'subjective state of well-being which minimises tension', and is regulated by norms common to a given social unit. The diffusion process may then be divided into four components: '(1) the innovation, and (2) its communication from one individual to another, (3) in a social system, (4) over time'.[22] Rogers uses the common distinction between inventors and adopters of new ideas, and regards the diffusion process as 'the spread of a new idea from its source of invention or creation to its ultimate users or adopters'.[23] Innovators are not necessarily inventors; they are the first, however, to adopt new ideas, and are looked on as 'deviants by other members of their social system'. Venturesomeness and cosmopolitanism are the basic values of innovators. Rogers follows Tarde, here, in believing that 'to innovate, to discover, to awake for an instant . . . the individual must escape, for the time being, from his social surroundings. Such unusual audacity makes him super-social rather than social'.[24] For Rogers, then, it is not the source or content or external context of origin of the invention which is important in diffusion, but the response in the recipient unit or 'system' with its dominant set of values and its fund of innovators. Similarly, it is the communicability of the innovation, and its simplicity and compatibility with the unit's established values and experiences, which are crucial for the rate at which it is adopted into the social system. Diffusion processes are therefore inserted in this approach into a systems framework by using Parsons' analysis of the elements of a unit act within a social system.[25]

Empirically, however, Rogers, like other innovation theorists, assigns to 'deviant' individuals a far greater role than was apparent in communications theory. But he fails to specify any mechanisms whereby some persons become more venturesome or cosmopolitan than others, except to characterise them as high status, often well-to-do individuals in close contact with sources of scientific innovation and with other innovators. But what are the social sources of the initial inventiveness and creativity at the root of innovation?

For many innovation theorists, the answer has been a version of the 'marginal man' thesis.[26] It is men who have not been sufficiently socialised into a given system and who are in some sense 'outsiders' (including ethnic or social minorities), who are most likely to compensate for their ambivalent status by creativity. The anxiety which accompanies the tensions inherent in their position in society, makes them prone to seek alternative and innovatory solutions.

An emphasis upon marginal individuals may take either a social or a more psychological form. The latter variant appears in the theories of Hagen, and especially McClelland, to explain the conditions of economic development and cultural innovation. Hagen argues that innovative personalities arise in families which have either stern fathers making excessive demands on their sons, or with weak fathers and nurturant mothers.[27] McClelland also claims that early training in mastery breeds a high need for achievement (n achievement) which in turn leads to entrepreneurial success.[28] At a collective level, Hagen locates the origins of deviant families in the withdrawal of respect, some generations earlier, from certain groups, often ethnic minorities, by elites after conquest or migration. McClelland's thesis is more psychological: there is a high correlation between national economic development and the earlier appearance of plays, songs and poems idealising heroic achievement.

In both versions of the thesis of child-rearing patterns, it is the deviant personality, acting outside established conventions, who becomes the main carrier of change. But it is not exactly micro-events which interest Hagen and McClelland, but an individual's values and need dispositions. Quite apart from the difficulties of making inferences from man's assumed internal states, to place the chief onus of social change or economic development on a certain type of personality is to risk minimising the impact of the social setting in which innovation occurs. Yet, for all the exaggeration of the role of personality in social change, the child-rearing thesis can be easily accommodated within a neo-evolutionist framework, since the creative values of the deviants emerge from the strains and tensions of heterogeneous social systems. To a neo-evolutionist such personality theses simply demonstrate that psychological factors and motivations are essential ingredients of a wider social process of economic development and social change.[29]

A much more explicit statement of the close links between diffusion and neo-evolutionism occurs in the theory of innovation advanced by LaPiere. Change, LaPiere claims, is abnormal and asocial: 'A change in society comes even as does a tumour in an organism, as a foreign and unwanted agent, not necessarily of destruction, but always of disturbance to the established and organisationally preferred structures and processes of life'.[30] Change violates the normal transmission of habits and standards over the generations, and is the product of crises and events which intrude from outside the system. Not all events produce change, and not all change is socially significant. Significant change involves the adoption of new external elements which events throw up, and that adoption is the work of deviants acting asocially against the inert structures of societies.

LaPiere's theory of social change falls into two parts. On the one hand there is the empirical study of innovation. Like Rogers, a distinction between invention and social innovation is drawn, and it is the position and characteristics of innovators and adopters that receives most attention.[31] In depicting change as asocial LaPiere has in mind what Park called the 'mass milling process', a situation in which numbers of individuals become desocialised, as in a crowd, and engage in 'mass milling'. Freed at least temporarily from constraints of family, neighbourhood and occupation, such individuals become receptive to new notions and techniques, and able to form spon-

taneous groupings to promote novelties. In all this LaPiere
appears to take issue with the neo-evolutionist idea that
change is normal and immanent in the unit or pattern undergoing it; for it requires the activities of men who stand in
some measure outside their society and its norms to induce
real, lasting change, and not some universal, unvarying social
law of change.

But the other side of LaPiere's thesis ties it firmly into
the neo-evolutionist framework. For the basis of his theory
of intrusive innovation is a model of society as a 'stable congruence' of functionally balanced elements. Societies which
approximate to this state, are in true social equilibrium and
have no need of change. Indeed, society for LaPiere may be
viewed as a self-maintaining process of social organisation
whose mode of operation is profoundly conservative. Not all
societies enjoy such freedom from disturbance. Some have
experienced a series of dysfunctions in their elements, which
in turn lead to chronic lack of congruence between the parts
of the system. This is the state of 'static incongruence', in
which there is chronic 'sickness': LaPiere cites Sicily and Spain
as examples. In these cases, there appears no way of breaking
the vicious circle to accommodate change and rectify the in-
congruencies between the parts, either because individuals
cannot be motivated for change or because the norms of the
society do not allow for it. It is only in societies experiencing
a state of 'dynamic incongruence', the open society, that dysfunctions can be modified through innovation from outside.
The organisation of such societies is open enough to accommodate significant change, and new elements can be inserted
into its organisation because it is sufficiently loose to allow
for modifications on an accumulative, piecemeal and planned
basis.[3 2]

Here we return to the major neo-evolutionist motif of
growth. It is the open, flexible, dynamic system that can incorporate change while retaining its basic structure, which
comes close to Eisenstadt's definition of modernisation, and

Bellah's insistence on rational flexibility. Equally neo-evolutionist is the idea of accumulative and piecemeal change; while the functionalist aspect reappears in LaPiere's model of congruence between the parts of a stable system. Where LaPiere, like Rogers or Hagen, differs from neo-evolutionism is in the specification of empirical processes of diffusion, which are, as it were, inserted into a broader neo-evolutionist framework. In this way, the neo-evolutionist framework itself is 'improved' on as a theory of historical change, while leaving its basic premises intact; for, without sacrificing its overall conception, 'neo-evolutionism with diffusion' becomes relevant to a wide range of historical problems and processes. Here again, we meet the apparent paradox of accommodation, even harmonisation, between two models whose sources of inspiration are radically opposed and whose empirical concerns are quite different.

Mass Movements

So far, the argument suggests that recent diffusion, that is, diffusion without diffusio*nism*, is theoretically dependent on other larger frameworks like the neo-evolutionist, and can offer no alternative view of the processes of historical change. In so far as many diffusion analysts explicitly or implicitly eschew any macro-theory of historical change, this conclusion is largely correct. From time to time, however, we encounter attempts to furnish a complete diffusionist alternative to other approaches, or at any rate to pose the problem of neo-evolutionist and diffusionist alternatives without seeking a resolution. Common to these attempts is a much more intense sense of the rupture and discontinuity of historical processes, of the impact of events, and of the role of human decisions, specific decisions at critical times, in those processes. In these schemes the key role is assumed by the concepts of intrusion and selection, particularly in the form of mass movements and ideologies.

Historians have often resorted to diffusionist explanations in dealing with political and cultural changes. The interplay of states in war and diplomacy and the fertilisation of cultures from alien sources still form an important part in some historical explanations of political or cultural changes within particular societies or ethnic groups. Moreover there have recently been deliberate attempts to set developments traditionally viewed as endogenous to given societies, for example the 1789 Revolution in France, in their wider continental or international context. Particular movements and changes become manifestations of a wider process or trend, such as Palmer envisages in his 'Atlantic' interpretation of the French Revolution, or Rude with his more Europe-oriented view.[33] Similarly with Nolte's comparative treatment of interwar French, Italian and German fascist movements, and Kornhauser's even broader 'mass society' interpretation of Nazism and communism as examples of an antidemocratic extremism which can engulf several societies during particular epochs.[34]

It should hardly surprise us therefore if historians of mass movements like nationalism and communism sometimes embrace a thorough-going diffusionism which views them as agents of subversion and destruction and seeks the mechanism of their importation on to virgin territory in the situation and activities of roaming intellectuals. An example of this ideological diffusionism is afforded by Trevor-Roper's account of European nationalism, whose eastward movement from the 'historic' cases of Germany, Italy and Hungary to the derivative 'secondary' examples in Eastern Europe he ascribes to the 'irresistible' power of the doctrine itself, mediated by the activities of the intelligentsia. For each of the small nationalities of Eastern Europe the mechanism of nationalism's diffusion has been the much-travelled, restless intellectual, who adopts the doctrine as much in reaction as in emulation of the earlier movements.[35]

This view of secular ideology as a 'great ideological impulse which burst the old framework of Europe in the nineteenth century',[3][6] can also be found in Kedourie's accounts of nation-alism. Kedourie ascribes to certain German philosophical dis-ciples of Kant, notably Fichte, Schlegel and Schleiermacher, a revolutionary power over the minds of romantic but rest-less younger generations in the bureaucratic, bourgeois and philistine communities from which they were spiritually and politically excluded. To such frustrated souls the message of national liberty and awakening seemed like the promise of the millennium on earth.[3][7] Kedourie in fact claims that nationalism is really a secular version of Christian millen-nialism, as it had developed from the prophecies of Joachim of Fiore to the Anabaptists. In the eighteenth century the ancient dream of man's perfectibility on a renovated earth appeared in secular garb, in Lessing's *Education of Humanity* (1780) and in the doctrine of evolutionary progress. It was soon adopted outside Europe. Intellectuals in Asia and Africa have all imbibed secular millennial doctrines promising free-dom and the good life once colonialism is destroyed and pro-gress harnessed to the needs of the masses. Kedourie likens this marxian nationalism to opiates which both soothe and excite their addicts to a frenzy of destruction, and he suggests that their course in history is inevitable and irresistible; for, having disrupted stable communities and traditions these ideological opiates appear to be able to satisfy man's need to belong in a stable society. Hence their appeal, which is matched only by their destructive effects.[3][8]

Although he does not follow the classical diffusionists in attempting a reconstruction of world history, Kedourie's account of modern revolution and change bears all the hall-marks of their approach. The source of change, secular mil-lennialism, is exogenous and intrusive. It is largely irresist-ible and it transforms existing patterns and units. It comes like an 'invasion', not of men, but of ideas and emotions, which upset orthodox ways and beliefs by claiming the superior power of science and reason over faith and revel-ation. What comes before this invasion and what follows are

85

utterly incommensurate; indeed, it is hard to talk of change in a given unit X or pattern Y, since these units and patterns are usually replaced by new ones. Moreover, Kedourie backs this view by appealing to the radical contingency of politics. In political and social affairs, chance rules and events upset well-ordered patterns and man's wisest calculations. New doctrines, like new religions, fall into this category of intrusive chance; they create, and are created by, the 'spirit of the age' which alone determines the outcome of man's actions. Men may try to select and adapt from a given ideology or movement what seems most apposite to the atavistic emotions of the masses, but ultimately they and their society succumb to the ideological and cultural spirit of their times.[39]

What Kedourie and other historians describe fits the pattern of explanation of change proposed by Teggart and adopted by Nisbet. Change they see as flowing from the impact of intrusive events—plagues, conquests, migrations or ideologies—which originate from an external source and wider context than that under investigation. In Teggart's view change results from the impact of different kinds of events situated in 'circles' which encompass that in which the unit under study is located, on that unit itself. Such change is normally accompanied by disruption of existing patterns and a crisis involving conflict between the old patterns and the intrusive new elements.[40] It is an essentially cataclysmic view of history and change, and as such appears to be much more apposite for an analysis of changes in a revolutionary era like our own.

Kedourie's formulation, however, reveals certain limitations in this view. To begin with, ideological diffusionism places an inordinate weight on the role of ideas in initiating and carrying through changes in social structures and institutions. Ideas are assumed to possess a coherence that they rarely in fact manifest; witness the numerous 'concessions' and 'adaptations' that even so highly elaborated a system as Marxism has made to 'local conditions' in different societies or in the hands of diverse strata.[4][1] Moreover, to deduce the spread of a given ideology to other lands from its inherent 'explosive' power is clearly question-begging. Why are some ideologies, out of the many that have been (or might be) elaborated, able to undermine traditional societies, and why do *they* exert an attraction? To appeal to the mechanisms of imitation or reaction to other elites again leaves unanswered the questions why it is *these* ideologies that are imitated, or *those* elites which are regarded as at once a standard of value and a threat to oneself.[4][2]

What all this suggests is that ideological diffusionism under-rates the creative, and selective, role of men in the processes of diffusion. Indeed, for all its emphasis upon chance in pub-lic life, this kind of diffusionism is quite as deterministic as many neo-evolutionary schemes. Only here it is powerful ideas, or *idées-forces*[4][3] which determine action, rather than the values and norms of a system, and the ideas burst into the existing patterns of the system rather than emanate from within. There are also more specific affinities between ideo-logical diffusionism and neo-evolutionism, in the parallel be-tween Kedourie's or Trevor-Roper's 'powerful ideas' and Smelser's 'generalised beliefs', or between the concept of successive epochs each with its own 'spirit', and Parsons's succession of cultural stages.

It is exactly against this excessive determinism, whether cultural as here or economic as in Marxist schemes, that a number of analysts have reacted. To be delivered from an endogenous determinism of evolutionary growth only to suc-cumb to an exogenous determinism of cataclysmic intrusions appears to them to bypass the essential problem posed by the historical record: the great variety of reactions and responses to a similar initial stimulus (always assuming, of course, that the stimuli are as similar as is often supposed), be it colonial-ism or capitalism, conquest or rationalism or superior tech-nology.

The variety of reactions and responses is particularly marked in the last few centuries. Societies in which a rationalist ethic, capitalism and industry have become prevalent, allow a far greater range of choice and opportunity, and involve a larger proportion of the population in the making of decisions. But this very freedom and heterogeneity carries dangers of disintegration or conflict, which can only be overcome through planning on behalf of the community. Hence the tendency for governments to engage in social experiment and welfare planning, and for social movements aiming at large-scale innovation to flourish in modern societies. This argument has recently been elaborated by Banks in his study of social movements.[44] His approach contrasts the neo-evolutionary functionalist study of unintended and unanticipated change with the more conscious, deliberate changes analysed by diffusionists like Rogers, Coleman and LaPiere.[45] Without prejudging the issue of their relationship, Banks finds the latter type of approach more fruitful for the understanding of social movements and their role in initiating change. This is particularly true of 'self-help' movements, which he defines as 'the deliberate creation of new social forms, run by the people themselves for themselves within the confines of existing societies and operating successfully as part of them'.[46] Such movements are characterised by an amalgam of old and new components; this

> combination of practices from the existing form of society with a novel element which will achieve a change in its form is what constitutes a social movement in the innovative sense, and it is to be emphasised that this was possible *only because social experimentation is commonplace in capitalist, industrial society.*[47] [italics in original].

In fact, Banks views all recent social movements, including workers' and revolutionary movements, as social technologies, to be interpreted in the same manner as the diffusion of technical inventions. A social movement may be regarded as a socially creative organisation which aims at constructive change, at deliberate innovation, in the existing social order, even where this involves a political revolution. Bank's main example is the Rochdale Society of Equitable Pioneers of 1844, and by extension, the world Co-operative Movement; and he singles out Charles Howarth's and William Cooper's ability to provide a synthesis of existing and new ideas, and advocate the founding of societies similar to their own.[48] Such processes of invention, advocacy and later adoption, which LaPiere had already distinguished, and the role networks that exist between people involved in such activities, are far more important, he maintains, than any personal characteristics of innovators, be they psychopathic as Heberle alleged at one point, or merely eccentric and nonconformist, as Gilfillan's study of imaginative creativity implies.[49] It is professional ties between innovators which diffuse inventions, and the similarity in attitudes of early adopters is largely a function of their sense of commitment and vocation.

Intrusion and selection

Central to this view of social change in the modern era, is the large role accorded to human choice and creativity. That is why Banks singles out social movements as one of the main motors of modern change and defines them in active, transitive terms. In this he follows a tradition stemming from Tonnies and Heberle, summed up in the recent definition by Wilkinson of social movement as 'a deliberate collective endeavour to promote change, having at least a minimal degree of organisation, and founded upon the normative commitment and active participation of followers or members'.[50] Both Banks and Wilkinson insist on the constructive and moral dimensions of many social movements, and contrast their approach with the 'natural history' framework favoured by Smelser and other functionalists, and by Kornhauser.[51] According to the latter view, social movements are seen as symptoms of disturbance in society, the end product of a long period of malaise and frustration building up into a col-

89

lective outburst or mass movement of frustrated and disoriented individuals. But Banks, like Killian and Heberle, insists that social movements are also creators of change and
not simply their creatures, for at every stage they involve
moral choices and mental innovation by leaders and followers
as they adapt their instrument of change to circumstances.
Social movements therefore do not simply emerge out of a
preceding undirected phase of 'inchoate groping towards the
collective consciousness', but direct that groping through a
new vision and new practices; for 'in societies where innovation of all kinds is a commonplace, the search for new forms
is an end in itself'.[5 2] That is why adherents of social movements reject conventions and existing social forms. It is not
just a sense of malaise or dissatisfaction with the *status quo*
which drives them to join movements, but a genuine convic-
tion of the need for change, and a commitment to new ideas
and forms of social relationship; in a word, a sense of vocation.

This leaves unanswered the question of the relationship
between creative engineered changes and the wider unintended
change so common in history. Banks's formulation highlights
this problem, since he argues that social movements are recent
innovations, and therefore for most of history, social changes
were unintended and unanticipated. Even today, many events
and much change do not result from the activities of a social
movement, as for example, with the social effects of technological change. So that intended and unintended changes may
often 'occur side by side'.[5 3] In this way, Banks's formulation
opens up a crucial issue which he does not attempt to resolve,
but argues for further research in this field.

Now, in opposing the broad, unintended change of the neo-
evolutionary functionalists to the more circumscribed deliberate changes dealt with by his own 'action frame of reference',
Banks in effect ignores a whole range of changes which fall
only in part within the latter category, and for which an
'action' approach is only partially satisfactory. For we may
divide the field of social changes into three main areas: first,

he cumulative, often quantitative changes like increase in iteracy, population or urbanisation—trends which neo-evolu-ionism may seek to explain; second, the smaller-scale, shorter-pan innovations with which an 'action theory' of social novements and creativity is concerned; and third, the medium-erm qualitative processes of exogenous change which have ended to form the subject-matter of both classical diffusion-sm and recent diffusion models, and which loom so large in he historical record.

As regards the larger part of historical changes the issue is not just, as Banks implies, between some form of structural volutionism on the one hand and a voluntaristic action frame f reference on the other. These are really only two extremes f a continuum of changes. The large middle ground of pro-esses of change is not dealt with adequately by either type f approach, at any rate in isolation. Social movements, which nay often last several generations and have enduring effects, re to be viewed neither as epiphenomena of differentiation r symptoms of strain, nor simply as technologies of diffusion nd instruments of realistic action, even though they may nvolve elements of both views. They are also disruptions nd agents of discontinuity with existing patterns and even units. They nearly always involve an intrusion on—a more or ess cataclysmic break with—the past. For all the determinism f his formulation, Kedourie is right to emphasise this revolu-ionary and external impact, which would liken a movement o a conquest or plague.

The crucial issue, then, is not so much between gradual umulative changes and the micro-events and innovations of ction theory, but between the role in human affairs of im-act and intrusion on the one hand, and ideals and selection n the other. Of course, a given process of historical change, nvolving large numbers and several decades, tends to be com-osed in varying measures of both kinds of element. The pro-lem is to discover some generalisations about their interrela-ions, to see how intrusion and selection are interwoven, and

accord due weight to each in different kinds of historical process. But before this can be done we need to recognise the
impact on a given pattern or unit of activities within other
patterns or units, and the way in which these activities help
to structure and initiate changes within the pattern or unit
under study. We need not view this exogenous relationship
wholly as one of unmitigated and unmediated intrusion, as
some historians and the early diffusionists have done, to be
convinced of the need to demarcate an important third field
of exogenous change, independent of both cumulative and
engineered changes.

Banks's formulation, therefore, for all its merits, does not
do full justice to the existence of this 'third field' of externally
originated, but nevertheless human and often creative change
nor to the complex interrelations between their impact and
intrusion and the creative selectivity and synthesis on the part
of members of the affected pattern or unit. In many types of
change, particularly of this processual kind, two sets of actors
are always involved: those in the external or 'foreign' pattern
or unit, be it institution or society, and those who are members of the institution or society or group under investigation
Similarly, two sets of interests, norms and activities are involved in most analyses of change in history. It is only at the
extremes of the continuum of changes, at the level of mankind or civilisation or religion or economy as such, or alternatively at the micro-level of small groups and clubs, that it may
be permissible to deal in terms of internally generated trends
or day-to-day events and a single set of actors and norms. But
in the vast majority of historical processes of change, with
which this book is concerned, the external reference is ignored at our peril; and the interplay of groups, institutions
and societies becomes the central preoccupation of any full-
scale theory of social change.

A concern with exogenous sources of change will also help
to restore the balance between ideology and practice in analysing social movements, which Banks's formulation some-

vhat impaired. For, by neglecting the impact of outside references and models, Banks and other action theorists underplay
he importance of selecting certain ideas and models as opposed to others which claim attention.[55] Resistance to some
mposed ideas is as vital as acceptance of others. Similarly
with foreign models of social organisation. Some cause more
disruption than others, some prove more acceptable than
others. Which kinds of models and ideas prove more attractive,
and why? How do these originate and spread? These questions
lead us to consider the sources of change, and especially the
role of ideas and models in initiating significant change.

6 Marx and Weber

The key issue of the relation between 'impact' and 'selection' is not confined to the debate between neo-evolutionists and diffusionists. It is also central to the continuing discussion between Marxists and Weberians on the role of ideas in social change. While comparisons of the views of the protagonists necessarily suffer from the fact that we are often dealing with scattered limbs of their work, only parts of which overlap, the debate which has arisen out of their work is particularly instructive for historical sociology. Of all the classical sociologists who have focused on problems of change, Marx and Weber are undoubtedly the most historically oriented, and hence most interested in the problems of selection, of situational impact and of external events, which we have repeatedly encountered. They are also most interested in the medium-term processes of discontinuous change which lead, not just to new levels and scales, but to new and qualitatively different forms.

There is another reason for devoting attention to their debate, namely, their interest in the origins of change, and the forces which initiate innovation. This is often summarised as an opposition of the role of ideas and interests in promoting change, but as we shall see, such a simplistic dichotomy misinterprets the aims and views of both Marx and Weber. On the other hand, the difference between Marx's more immanentist and structuralist conception of historical change and Weber's more exogenist evential interpretation, has sometimes been underplayed or misrepresented. The fact remains that both were particularly concerned with the locus of change, as much indeed as the diffusionist has focused on the channels of that change, or the neo-evolutionist on its consequences. This does not mean that Marx and Weber were uninterested in consequences and forms of change. The reverse is true; it is the forms from which they set out, the general direction that Marx finds in human history, the particular values that Weber discovers embedded in the several culture histories of mankind. Moreover, both Marx and Weber are interested in the mechanisms by which changes percolate through a society, particularly in the classes and strata which act as carriers or promoters of change. Nevertheless their main contribution to the study of historical changes lies in their approach and hypotheses on the sources and impetus of processes of change; and the differences in their approach highlight the difficulties of endogenous models of social change.

Class contradiction and consciousness

The questions posed at the end of the last chapter, as to how new ideas and models originate and prove widely attractive, may serve as a convenient point of departure. For Marx, ideas and ideologies express the goals and perceptions of men as they interact with the world and with each other. It is active and creative men who elaborate conceptions and visions of their activity and of the world in which their activity takes place. As Marx puts it in *The German Ideology*: 'Consciousness is therefore from the very beginning a social product, and remains so as long as men exist at all'.[1] Ideas and conceptions have no independent origin or causal force, but arise only in conjunction with the activities, the 'practical-critical' activity, of men engaged in revolutionising the contradictions in their social environment. Such practical consciousness is an essential characteristic of man as opposed to animals: it defines his life-process, and his humanity, what Marx calls man's

95

'species-being' (*Gattungswesen*), a term which recalls Feuerbach's view of man.[2] Only for Marx man's humanity is historically conditioned. As a result, his activity and thought, too, are subject to historical change and development. It is culture, along with social activity, which distinguishes men from animals, and since culture and society are constantly changing, the content of man's humanity also changes and progresses, along with, and partly as a result of, his practical consciousness.[3]

The insistence on creative, practical consciousness as man's essential characteristic, separates Marx's historicist view of social change from a purely materialist doctrine. For materialism opposes a realm of material facts and relations to a complementary spiritual one, and derives the latter, more or less mechanically, from the former. But Marx considers that 'circumstances are changed by men', and that 'the coincidence of the change of circumstances and of human activity or self-change can be comprehended and rationally understood only as *revolutionary practice*'.[4] [italics in original]. This fusion of thought and action by men modifies society in two main ways: through productive activity or work, and through political activity or revolution. It is through production that men influence history on a day-to-day basis, since, as a result of the division of labour which productive activity has encouraged from the earliest times, men become increasingly alienated both from the objects of their labour and from their work activity itself. The worker is, accordingly, stripped progressively of his 'species-being' and approximates that of the animals, even as wealth accumulates in the hands of property owners. The result of productive activity is, therefore, an intensification of class antagonism within the existing type of productive process and the corresponding kind of society. Second, when class conflict can no longer be maintained, criticism becomes translated into political action by members of the downtrodden class. In this way, the ruling conceptions of the society are challenged, in theory and in practice, by a revolutionary current of thought and activity on the part of members of the alienated class. Together, work and revolution force society to change, and bring about the transcendence (*Aufhebung*) of one form of economy and society by another.[5]

If, therefore, we ask what constitutes the source and impetus for historical change for Marx, we must conclude that it is neither ideas, nor 'material forces' as such, but simply men who have become conscious of their situation in history and whom that situation, coupled with the characteristics of their 'species-being', impels to seek a revolutionary change in their condition. Historical change always arises from this dialectical relationship between *homo faber* and his conscious practical activity, and the given situation in which he finds himself. For men make revolutions, but not simply as and when they please. Even to conceive of a revolutionary upheaval requires a clear perception of the contradictions of their situation; for the revolution to have any chance of success requires, in addition, a whole series of appropriate conditions, superimposed and in a determinate sequence.[6]

It is at this point that some of the ambiguities and tensions of the Marxist view of historical change become apparent. For, on the one hand, 'the whole of what is called world history is nothing but the creation of man by human labour'[7]; on the other, it is the struggle for scarce resources to satisfy collective needs, which impels men to specialise so as to produce more wealth and support a growing population.[8] The division of labour, in turn, is the basis, both of class divisions and private property. The changing relationship between property and class relations on the one hand, and technological and organisational progress on the other, provide the fundamental contradictions which generate social change. Over and again, Marx emphasizes that 'material conditions' condition or even determine the activity of individuals.[9] Men, through activity and production, help to shape their circumstances; yet they are 'effective, produce materially, and are active under

97

definite material limits, presuppositions and conditions independent of their will'.[10]

The point is that though men modify their situations, they start out from situations which have been shaped by preceding generations and have assumed a definite and crystallised form. That form, once tribal society has passed, is always based on opposition of classes underpinned by an all-embracing division of labour. The division of labour coerces men and distorts their relation to both the objects of their work and their fellow human beings; it also determines a man's position in society. For a man's occupation places him at once into a clear relationship to productive activity, and the means by which men produce. It determines whether he will be able to appropriate the wealth that men produce, or only toil to produce without use or benefit thereof. Hence the division of labour brings private property in its train, and leads also to the separation of town and country, and to the division of men into antagonistic classes, each pursuing its own interest.[11]

Occupational position, therefore, the place that men occupy in a determinate process of production, generates social conflicts and coercive relations between groups of men, irrespective of individual will. Hence the origin of social change, as well as of social inertia, must be sought in changing economic functions. But new functions arise on the basis of technological and organisational improvements, just as old functions may be retained through the interests of the dominant class in a given occupational order. Hence change is always dialectical and asynchronous as between the analytically separable sectors of man's life. It proceeds, first, from a clash between technological progress and the constraints of an existing class and property structure; and secondly, from the conflict between two polar interest-classes occupying diametrically opposed positions in the existing hierarchy of labour. In this second source of change ideas and conscious activity play a large role: for, to carry on a class conflict, the oppressed (as well as the oppressor) must become aware of its unity of nterests and create political organisations and a leadership capable of challenging the ruling class's monopoly of State power.[12] Hence the contradictions which arise out of the division of labour and private property lead inevitably to social revolution, through the mediating influence of class conflict. Only revolution can, at least temporarily, abolish the contradictions between an obsolete and innovatory mode of production, between the new mode of production and the old class structure, and between the ruling and subject classess. Hence, 'it is only in an order of things in which there are no more classes and class antagonisms that social evolutions will cease to be political revolutions'.[13]

Charisma and rationalisation

Marx's theory of social change presents a unified model in which the several contradictions between the parts of a 'system' of social existence generate periodic transformations of that system. Successive forms of social existence or 'socio-economic formations' manifest a similar general form or relationship between the parts, although their content and intensity varies. Marx believed that we can ascribe a rational meaning to this historical process of social self-transcendence, a definite pattern of social development which unfolds universal values at the end of its often turbulent course. Whereas capitalism as the first universal mode of production carries mass alienation to its extreme, communism, in which the universal class of the proletariat abolishes its own and 'thereby also every other previous mode of appropriation',[14] restores to man his essential humanity, his true consciousness, shorn of the contradictions and distortions nurtured by a stultifying division of labour. Hence 'the bourgeois relations of production are the last antagonistic form of the social process of production . . . the closing chapter of the prehistoric stage of human society'.[15]

Whereas Marx's theory of social change presents two clear

tendencies within a tension of opposites, a more activistic conception and a more structuralist one, such that radically different interpretations become possible, the Weberian approach hardly permits of a unified theory of historical change at all. Whereas in Marx the problem is to balance and integrate earlier and later emphases and formulations round a core whose central thrust is emphatically clear, with Weber it is a question of selecting out of many separate analyses of social changes a central focus and arriving at some more general framework to guide those analyses. Nevertheless certain ideas recur like leitmotives throughout Weber's work, and our original question as to the origin and diffusion of ideas in social change provides again a convenient starting-point.

Weber agrees with Marx that man is an essentially creative being. But he is creative in a special sense; not in his material production but in his creation of values. With every decision he makes, man affirms one set of values and denies another. But decisions, in turn, which form the basis of behaviour, are explicable largely in terms of conceptions of the world, images of existence, held by the actor. Values then are the product of freely chosen beliefs about the world and our place in it. Of course, men do not choose any set of beliefs, nor is their choice free from limitations. In fact, there are a number of factors which influence choice, some 'ideal' and others 'material'. Among the former are the prevailing images of the world crystallised, usually, in religious conceptions, but increasingly today in secular ideologies or 'religion surrogates'. For Weber, such religious conceptions and systems stem from a primitive sense of the sacred object or person, the 'extraordinary' quality which Weber terms *charisma*.[16] This quality represents a break with everyday life, with the world of ordinary things, and is viewed by Weber as strictly 'irrational' from the standpoint of every existing conception and habit. It is here then that we must locate the primary source of value change, and hence a considerable factor in broader social change.

Weber defines charisma, in the first place, as an attribute of persons. It is a 'certain quality of an individual personality by virtue of which he is set apart from ordinary men and treated as endowed with supernatural, superhuman, or at least specifically exceptional powers or qualities'.[17] It does not matter whether the individual actually possesses the qualities attributed to him; for 'what is alone important is how the individual is actually regarded by those subject to charismatic authority, by his "followers" or "disciples" '.[18] Although guaranteed by 'signs' and 'proofs', often in the form of miracles or revelations, charisma is basically a matter of personal devotion, a sense of awe and reverence, of inclusion in something conceived to be extraordinary (*aussertäglich*) and to embody a supraindividual purpose. Although, too, charisma attaches, not merely to men, but to offices, institutions and orders, especially in the process by which charisma is returned to everyday life, the 'routinisation of charisma' (*Veralltäglichung des Charismas*), the personal element of mystic devotion remains for Weber prototypical. It is largely this affective, irrational element which confers an unpredictable instability on charismatic intrusions on the normal course of events. Founded on a devotion 'born of distress and enthusiasm', charismatic domination

'is revolutionary and transvalues everything; it makes a sovereign break with all traditional or rational norms: "It is written, but I say unto you" '.[19]

One result of charismatic intrusions is a rejection of every type of development theory of history. Another is the reinforcement of Weber's characteristic view of historical analysis as one of ascertaining relations that are probable rather than determinate.

But, of course, charisma, though its content and intensity cannot be wholly explained by reference to either material or ideal factors, always takes place within a historical situation composed of contingent sequences of events, which we analyse

101

into separate 'factors' or causal chains. Among these factors three stand out as recurrent themes in Weber's discussions: abstraction and intellectualism, authority relations and the role of classes and status groups.

The first of these is part of the more general process of rationalisation which Weber discerned in history, and more especially in Western civilisation. In one sense, rationalisation is simply a consequence of successive charismatic 'break-throughs', usually in the form of prophetic annunciations. Prophetism brings a 'systematic and coherent meaning' to the society and the cosmos, sees the cosmos indeed as a 'meaningful, ordered totality', to which 'the conduct of mankind must be oriented if it is to bring salvation'.[20] This is one sense of rationalisation: the achievement of a system of concepts and beliefs which has inner consistency, even when founded on illogical premises (illogical, that is, from the standpoint of modern science). Another allied sense is the submission of all conduct to a unified plan and programme viewed as a means to an absolute end. Both are consequences of the systematisation of the prophetic message by intellectuals whose need for salvation is more inward, 'more remote from life, more theoretical and more systematic than salvation from external distress'.[21] Between them, prophets and intellectuals destroy magic: hence 'the world's processes become disenchanted, lose their magical significance, and henceforth simply "are" and "happen" but no longer signify anything'.[22] At this point, intellectualism becomes a causal factor in its own right. At first, it was the case that

> In all times there has been but one means of breaking down the power of magic and establishing a rational conduct of life; this means the great rational prophecy. ... Prophecies have released the world from magic and in doing so have created the basis for our modern science and technology, and for capitalism.[23]

At a later stage, intellectualism, by pushing to its limits the problem of meaning raised by religious theodicies, provides the basis for secular civilisations in its own right, in the form

102

of science, displacing religion altogether. We see the process, especially, in the secularisation of Calvinism through increasing rationalisation. Life becomes wholly utilitarian and instrumental now: 'It means that principally there are no mysterious incalculable forces that come into play, but rather that one can, in principle, master all things by calculation. This means that the world is disenchanted'.[24]

A second set of factors entering the historical milieu in which charisma intrudes, is constituted by existing authority relations. Usually these are traditional, based on the 'sanctity of the order and the attendant powers of control as they have been handed down from the past, "have always existed".'[25] More recently, we meet another type of legitimation for authority, the rational-legal kind, whose chief expression is the organised bureaucracy of paid officials, bound by fixed rules and impersonal relations. In many ways, the bureaucratisation of the state is the single most important element in the overall process of rationalisation; but on the whole it appears as a massive consequence or process of historical change, a diffusion process of the rationalist spirit and capitalist economy, rather than an initiator of social change, except very recently. In fact, authority systems tend to be viewed by Weber, along with ritual and magic, as socially conservative forces. There is one important exception; the military hero and, more generally, conquest. Thus, discussing the origins of seigniorial proprietorship, Weber lays some emphasis on conquest and submission to the military leader as among the bases for a landed 'class of overlords'.[26] Similarly, international power conflicts form an important set of conditions for the rise of Israelite prophecy, and even for its specific concerns and message.[27] Conquest, too, and more generally 'political action', plays a vital part in the formation of ethnic groups which share common memories of decisive political events and have been moulded by common struggles against other groups.[28] Here then, competing power groups embodying different sets of cultural values exercise considerable influ-

103

ence on social change, both directly and through the conceptions of charismatic heroes, even if in both cases the resulting change is unanticipated and unintended.

Among the chief kinds of competing groups, classes and status groups stand out as a third set of factors composing different historical situations. Indeed, so much attention does Weber give to the role of such strata, particularly in the city, that some have even argued that ideas 'would seem to emanate for the most part from class interest'.[29] Certainly Weber wavers on this point, despite his protestations:

> This is a highly checkered diversification, which at least proves that a uniform determinism of religion by economic forces never existed among the artisan class. Yet there is apparent in these lower middle classes, in contrast to the peasantry, a definite tendency towards congregational religion, towards religion of salvation, and finally towards rational ethical religion. But this contrast between the middle class and the peasantry is far from implying any uniform determinism.[30]

Nevertheless, Weber does present a mechanism by which class interest is related to ideas in a systematic, yet non-deterministic manner. Through the concept of 'elective affinity', individuals and groups are viewed as choosing which ideas and beliefs to follow, while at the same time their life-styles predispose them to elect certain kinds of beliefs and reject others, through an affinity between that life-style and particular images of the world. In this way, the life-style of peasants inclines them towards magic, and chivalrous warriors have been attracted by the idea of fate and destiny.[31] Similarly,

> it is still true in theory that the middle class, by virtue of its distinctive pattern of economic life, inclines in the direction of rational ethical religion . . . the economic foundation of the urban man's life has a far more rational essential character, viz., calculability and capacity for purposive manipulation . . . small traders and artisans are disposed to accept a rational world view incorporating an ethic of compensation.[32]

It is for these reasons that Weber concludes that man's conduct, and hence historical change which is significant, depends in the final analysis on three analytically separable sets of factors: the constellation of material interests of a stratum, both economic and political; ideas, which become systematised and intellectualised into 'images of the world' and which take a stand in the face of the world; and finally, the 'ideal interests' of a stratum or group (class, status group or power group like a nation) by which it defines its situation in the world, both as it is and as it 'should' ideally be. Speaking of the rationalisation of the idea of redemption into a coherent 'image of the world', Weber summarises his view of the role of the latter in social change:

> Not ideas, but material and ideal interests, directly govern men's conduct. Yet very frequently the 'world images' that have been created by 'ideas' have, like switchmen, determined the tracks along which action has been pushed by the dynamic of interest. 'From what' and 'for what' one wished to be redeemed and, let us not forget, 'could be' redeemed, depended upon one's image of the world.[33]

Origins of capitalism

In presenting in schematic outline some of the main ideas of Marx and Weber on the origins of change, I am concerned less with a comparison of their views and standpoints (a task excellently treated elsewhere),[34] than with an attempt to locate and assess their different responses to this question of origins, in the light of two continuing debates: the problem of voluntarism, and the issue of exogeneity. The first of these debates is very much at the root of the discussions between Marxists and Weberians; the second is somewhat more peripheral to their concerns and therefore involves a more critical assessment of their different responses. Since capitalism, albeit in differing aspects, became for Weber as well as Marx a central problem area and testing-ground for historical analysis, this affords a convenient locus for comparison as the only well-documented case studied by both.

105

As has been noted by several authors, the treatment of the problem of capitalism's emergence is broadly similar in the work of Marx and Weber. Both set out from a demarcation of modern Western capitalism from other non-Western types. Weber calls the former 'sober bourgeois capitalism' to distinguish it from trading, adventurer or political types of capitalism, which have always existed. Marx too felt that modern capitalism is a recent historical development: 'The passion for wealth is a distinctive development: ... the thirst for self-enrichment is the product of a definite social development; it is not natural, but historical'.[35] Both underlined the ascetic character of rational capitalism, its rejection of enjoyment in order to maximise profit, to accumulate money for its own sake and without limit. Commodity production for Marx presupposes not merely money, but an unnatural renunciation for investment, which is the basis for Weber of that rational calculability, epitomised in double-entry book-keeping, which is the hallmark of modern capitalism.[36] Marx also agrees with Weber that modern capitalism presupposes a class of legally free wage-earners, an uprooted and alienated proletariat, who sell their labour on the commodity market.[37] There is also an important difference: Marx emphasises the class contradiction of the capitalist system, whereas Weber singles out the element of technical expertise and rational discipline—capitalism's peculiar ethos and institutional norms.

There are also broad similarities in the treatment of the origins of capitalism, despite the celebrated controversey over the causal role of Calvinist asceticism. Both envisage the development of capitalism as a long-drawn-out process starting with the growth of free towns in the eleventh century as centres of mercantile activity, relatively free from feudal and ecclesiastical restrictions. For Marx, the communal movement of the twelfth and thirteenth centuries and the expropriation of the peasantry, especially in sixteenth- and seventeenth-century England (where enclosures

later drove masses of landless labourers into urban industrial production), greatly accelerated the drive towards 'primary accumulation' by individual producers who become entrepreneurs and increasingly manage their estates on a commercial basis.[39] Weber acknowledges the development of
many features of capitalist enterprise in the later Middle
Ages, especially in Italy, but adds that the ethos of capitalism required the dynamism provided by the Reformation
and especially the Puritan work ethic. The real impetus to
business activity was furnished by the marked psychological uncertainty over the attainment of salvation in the minds
of Calvinists who accepted doctrines of predestination and
stewardship. This uncertainty forced the merchant believer
to look for signs of divine grace in terrestrial success. Com-
manded to do good works, to build God's kingdom in Geneva
or Amsterdam, he came to interpret his worldly success as a
sign of divine election, and to regard his activity as a God-
given 'vocation'. In this way, a new conception of the world
(Calvinism) determined the direction of merchant interests
by providing a new ethic of work and renunciation, which
ennobled a stratum hitherto despised in a predominantly aristocratic society.[40]

Yet, for all this emphasis on a specific hypothesis and
mechanism, the Weberian account shares much common
ground with the Marxist. In his later studies of the economic
ethic of the major world religions, Weber increasingly emphasised the freedoms of the Western type of city from family,
religious and political restrictions. He also accentuated the
economic and political factors which prevented the development of capitalism in China and India, despite some favourable conditions.[41] Moreover, Weber's concept of 'elective
affinity' between ideas and the life-styles of certain strata, is
not so distant from the Marxist notion of a reciprocity of
influence between the economic interests of the bourgeoisie
and their typical conceptions of the world, as in the case

where Marx relates the idea of parliamentary democracy to the mode of life and activity of petty bourgeois shopkeepers in France.[42]

Where Marx and Weber differ is in the degree to which they locate the origins and development of capitalism either within the pre-existing (feudal) system or in external influences and events; and coupled with this, the latitude which they extend to the perceptions and decisions of individuals and groups. Broadly speaking, Marx's account is preponderantly 'immanentist', and far less voluntaristic than Weber's. His analysis of the rise of capitalism in Western Europe acknowledges, it is true, the importance of specific historical circumstances. Thus, when asked whether his account of primary accumulation in *Capital* could apply outside the West, and particularly to Russia, Marx emphasised the differences between analogous historical developments situated in various countries and periods. Citing the example of the Roman proletarians who had been expropriated from their landholdings and became, not wage labourers, but a 'mob of do-nothings', he warns:

> Thus events strikingly analogous but taking place in different historical surroundings led to totally different results. By studying each of these forms of evolution separately and then comparing them one can easily find the clue to this phenomenon, but one will never arrive there by using as one's master key a general historico-philosophical theory, the supreme virtue of which consists in being super-historical.[43]

Nevertheless, it is just such a theory, or rather 'image' of social development, which forms the 'guiding thread' for his investigations. Even if we regard it as nothing more than a hypothesis and method of analysis, its hold in Marx's account is so strong that other causal chains which one might consider as important as peasant expropriation in the emergence of capitalism are treated as purely contributory or additional factors. Behind this 'hypothesis' stands a distinctive metaphor, that of internal growth. Thus, in the same letter, Marx writes:

> The chapter on primitive accumulation does not pretend to do more

than trace the path by which, in Western Europe, the capitalist order of economy emerged from the womb of the feudal order of economy. It therefore describes the historical movement which by divorcing the producers from their means of production converts them into wage workers (proleterians in the modern sense of the word) while it converts those who possess the means of production into capitalists.[44]

In other words, the choice of historical hypothesis and its overriding importance as against other factors and hypotheses has been determined by a particular image of social change as emerging from within an existing self-contradictory structure and from a particular philosophical thesis about subject-object interaction breeding alienation, again within a largely self-contained unit, an entity conceived as necessarily self-realising through dialectical development. It is this same immanentist image of necessary development which underlies Marx's overall conception of historical change in the famous Preface to *A Contribution to the Critique of Political Economy*:

No social order [he writes], ever disappears before all the productive forces for which there is room in it have been developed, and new, higher relations of production never appear before the material conditions of their existence have matured in the womb of the old society.[45]

The same metaphor of development, both in its organic and in a more mechanistic form, appears in other passages such as the Preface to the first edition of *Capital*, in which Marx declares that his aim is to study 'the economic law of motion of modern society', and that the 'evolution of the economic formation of society is viewed as a process of natural history'.[46] No such image informs Weber's analysis. This is not to say that Weber does not operate normally in terms of events occurring within a particular unit such as the West, China and India; only he is far more aware of the contingent relations between different sectors such as the economy, polity and religious beliefs within very broad entities like civilisations. Marx's immanentism in his analysis of capitalism is dual: he traces the emergence of one economic order from (out of) another pre-existent one, as well as from within the

109

economic order of a given country like England or France. By contrast, Protestantism for Weber, whatever its origins, acts as a transnational and cross-cultural movement affecting the whole of western, central and northern Europe. Marx, of course, is perfectly aware of external intrusions which hasten or delay capitalist accumulation and peasant expropriation; witness his remarks on the dissolution of monasteries in England and the effect of the discovery of America and the East Indies.[47] At the same time, such intrusive sequences of events are no more than catalysts of a process already forming in the economic contradictions of the old order. Whereas it is of the essence of Weber's method and approach that such intrusive event sequences are *necessary* conditions of those under investigation in another sector or region of social life. So Calvin's sense of divine mission is not just a catalyst of capitalist development, but a precondition, because its unintended consequence was a change in merchant self-conceptions which fostered the 'spirit of capitalism', itself an essential ingredient of the capitalist social order.[48]

Such a partial exogenism is allied to Weber's emphasis on personal choice by the participants. This in turn stems from his radical dissociation of factual and normative propositions, between scientific analysis and value judgments. Ideals and values are irreducible and fundamentally irrational. Indeed the highest ideals 'are always formed only in the struggle with other ideals which are just as sacred to others as ours are to us'.[49] For Weber, life knows only of 'an unceasing struggle of these gods with one another. Or speaking directly, the ultimately possible attitudes towards life are irreconcilable ... Thus it is necessary to make a decisive choice'.[50] Not only individuals, but every kind of group—class, status group, ethnic group, nation—has irreconcilable beliefs and values which struggle for ascendancy over the minds and hearts of individuals. That is why the different ideals of conduct which influence personal choice in the great world religions so preoccupy Weber and why he traces the psychological effects of their world views and ethics, considering that they have as much bearing on action as class or status position. At the same time, there is more than a suspicion of a partial cultural determinism here, since individuals are often portrayed as driven by, or at least, permeated with, a given ideal, often at birth, especially in more traditional cultures.[51]

Marx allows far less latitude for personal commitment and the influence of ideals and values. Both capitalists and proletarians are equally subject to the class values generated by their respective positions in the system of commodity production. Similarly, the class structure determines which ideas will become prominent and dominant in society. Usually, the ruling ideas are those of the dominant class who control intellectual production; but, in revolutionary periods like the transition to capitalism, classes arise which take up radical ideas with which to challenge the hegemony of the ruling class.[52] So the bourgeoisie in 1789 adopted 'Roman costume' and 'Roman phrases' for its social and economic task, while Cromwell and the English 'borrowed speech, passions and illusions from the Old Testament for their bourgeois revolution'.[53] Everywhere Marx contrasts the 'real' task and aim of classes with their own conception of what they are doing. The latter is 'illusory' in the sense of being a partial class interest, whereas in their conception the aim becomes universal. But it is also illusory in the sense that will and subjective ideals are based on and grow out of the 'real foundation' of material conditions, but in a partial and necessarily distorted manner. Even 'civil society', that is, the form of intercourse and relations between men, is historically created by the 'simple material production of life', even if the 'productive forces' are modified by successive generations. Each generation has 'prescribed for it its conditions of life', its 'definite development, a special character', so that 'circumstances make men just as much as men make circumstances'.[54]

Applied to capitalism, this historical materialism relegates the individual to a position of dependence on the relations of

111

production, 'whose creature he socially remains, however
much he may subjectively raise himself above them'.[55] The
'natural laws of capitalist production' provide the framework
of Marx's analysis. Hence, 'it is a question of these laws themselves, of these tendencies working with iron necessity towards inevitable results. The country that is more developed
industrially only shows, to the less developed, the image of
its own future'.[56] In the Preface to the second edition of
Capital, Marx strengthens the impression of subordinating
individual will to economic laws of development, by quoting
with approval a critic who explains that Marx's aim is

> to show, by rigid scientific investigation, the necessity of successive
> determinate orders of social conditions, and to establish, as impar-
> tially as possible, the facts that serve him for fundamental starting
> points. For this it is quite enough if he proves, at the same time, the
> necessity of the present order of things and the necessity of another
> order, into which the first must inevitably pass over; and this all the
> same, whether men believe or do not believe it, whether they are
> conscious or unconscious of it. Marx treats the social movement as
> a process of natural history, governed by laws not only independent
> of human will, consciousness and intelligence, but rather, on the
> contrary, determining that will, consciousness and intelligence.[57]

And the critic whom Marx considers 'pictures' the 'dialectic
method' of *Capital*, adds:

> In a word, economic life offers us a phenomenon analogous to the
> history of evolution in other branches of biology . . . . The scientific
> value of such an inquiry lies in the disclosing of the special laws that
> regulate the origin, existence, development and death of a given
> social organism and its replacement by another and higher one.

Even if we accept Marx's claim that the discovery of such laws
arises out of inductive and detailed historical inquiry, there is
little doubt that it also serves not just as a framework for inquiry but also as a master-principle of explanation to which
other possible hypotheses, and specially those starting out
from the conceptions of individuals, are completely subord-
inated. In fact the 'guiding thread' which confers such primacy

on production in social and intellectual life proceeds as much from Marx's revolutionary philosophy of history, his commitment to an ethic of 'ultimate ends', as from his detailed historical analyses.[5][8]

Ideology and revolution

In tracing the origins of capitalism, Marx and Weber take up the problems posed by what both agree is a long-term historical trend, whose explanandum is largely economic. Their differences of interpretation, particularly over the issues of exogenism and voluntarism, become even more marked when they discuss the medium- and short-term political and cultural changes, even though here their writings cannot be directly compared. Weber did not get round to writing his chapter on political revolution, and Marx's comments on artistic and intellectual changes are sporadic. Nevertheless it is possible to reconstruct, to some extent, their general approaches to these vital kinds of change.

For Marx the political sphere derives from 'civil society', the social relations which men form in production, especially from private ownership. The modern bureaucratic state is, likewise, not Hegel's 'universal class', nor does it represent the common interest of selfish sectional groups; rather it expresses the class interests of those who have appropriated the surplus of a given set of productive forces.[5][9] Hence the political sector provides an additional set of instruments for coercing and exploiting the propertyless, who, if they wish to challenge the owners, must seize the organs of the state and establish a new administrative order on the ruins of the old.

From these premises, Marx's theory of revolution unfolds as the culmination of a series of 'contradictions' and class conflicts between, first, feudal lords and bourgeois, and later, the bourgeoisie and the proletariat. The starting-point of the process is a growing antagonism between the 'forces' and 'relations' of production, between the changing technology and organisation of that production and the class and property relations which impede those changes. As Marx says:

> At a certain stage of their development the material forces of production in society come into conflict with the existing relations of production, or—what is but a legal expression for the same thing—with the property relations within which they had been at work before. From forms of development of the forces of production, these relations turn into their fetters. Then comes the period of social revolution. With the change of the economic foundation the entire immense superstructure is more or less rapidly transformed.[60]

Applied to the demise of capitalism, this means that the concentration and centralisation of capital diminishes the number of competing capitalists and expropriates ever growing numbers of workers into an industrial reserve army. Factory production and the misery of their degraded existence gradually welds this mass into a class, conscious of its situation and unity of interest. Hence:

> The monopoly of capital becomes a fetter upon the mode of production which has sprung up and flourished along with and under it. Centralisation of the means of production and socialisation of labour at last reach a point where they become incompatible with their capitalist integument. This integument is burst asunder. The knell of capitalist private property sounds. The expropriators are expropriated. ... But capitalist production begets, with the inexorability of a law of nature, its own negation. It is the negation of negation.[61]

The upshot of this argument is, first, that political change and revolution emerges directly from economic changes and contradictions, as these become polarised in class conflict; and second, that no political change can be successful unless the economic and social conditions for it are 'ripe'. The French Revolution in a case in point. Here Marx discerns two separate revolutions: that of 1789, when the bourgeoisie overthrew the feudal seigneurs and freed economic activity from political and status restrictions, that is they freed civil society from the state; and that of 1793-94, when the Jacobins and sans-culottes took advantage of political terror to promote a proletarian revolution which was bound to fail in the absence of factory production and a sizeable force of wage-earners. The revolution of 1793-94 was premature and purely political. Political will and activism are no substitute for the social and economic conditions which foster an organised proletariat. Even proletarian praxis and radicalism of a Roux or Blanqui require the corresponding material conditions if they are to eventuate in social revolution. As Marx put it in an article of 1847:

> If the proletariat brings down the domination of the bourgeoisie, its victory will be merely ephemeral, only a moment in the service of the bourgeoisie (just like *anno* 1794), so long as within the process of history, within its 'movement', those material conditions have not been created that make necessary the abolition of the bourgeois mode of production and therefore also the definitive fall of the bourgeois political domination.[62]

Marx's remarks on the French Revolution contain the germ of the 'theory of the bourgeois revolution', by which Marxian historians have explained the origins and course of the revolutionary era in late eighteenth century France.[63] Recently that interpretation has been subjected to some searching criticisms, notably for its tendency to derive the political struggles of factions, especially in Paris, from largely economic factors mediated through 'class' conflicts. In particular, the standard Marxist equation of the political representatives of the *tiers etat*, called the bourgeois, with the social class of either rentier proprietors (the bourgeois proper) or Marx's usual meaning of the bourgeoisie, the financiers, entrepreneurs and especially the industrialists, has been questioned. Similarly, with the terms 'nobles' and 'feudalism', which, like the concept of the bourgeoisie, cover a number of different groupings and strands, only some of which were active in the political revolutions. The driving force in the latter were the professional intelligentsia, especially the lawyers, and the declining stratum of *officers*, members of the royal administration; whereas the rentiers tended to be conservative, and the financiers and entrepreneurs took little part in the political fray (though they were pitted against the *officiers* in various municipal commercial struggles).[64]

The general tendency of this critique of the theory of a 'bourgeois revolution' is in line with Weber's well-known insistence on the parity between political power and economic property as joint and irreducible determinants, along with world-images, of social action, including radical rebellions. This is partly because action is also governed by shared beliefs in the legitimacy of authority relations, partly because the 'threat and application of physical force' in a defined territory is a guarantee of order and hence material benefits, provided it is monopolised by the legitimate authority.[65] Weber, in other words, wishes to retain for the political sphere a considerable autonomy. But at the same time he aims to show the impact of the political on the ideal and material spheres, and vice versa.

Thus an important 'starting-point' in Weber's examination of the social structure of the ancient Israelite confederacy and the rise of urbanism in Palestine is the fact of external conquest by an unstable confederation of tribal peasants and small stock breeders. Political factors like conquest and exile, also serve as preconditions of the diaspora situation of Jewry as a 'guest' or 'pariah' people. Above all, political danger forms the essential context of classical Israelite prophecy:

> Except for the world politics of the great powers which threatened their homeland and constituted the message of their most impressive oracles, the prophets could not have emerged . . .
> Free prophecy developed only with the rising external danger to the country and to the royal power.[66]

The ancient prophets of Israel are the type of charismatic revolutionary. Not that their intention is revolutionary, nor do they organise a party or sect: indeed 'Precisely in solitude did the prophetic spirit come', and they spoke to an often hostile audience. Their attitude to social problems and politics was 'purely religious in motivation', yet Weber considers them a status group of 'world-political demagogues and publicists', even if they had no political intentions.[6][7] Socially too, their origins are diverse. They receive support, neither from the peasants nor the kings or priests, but their prophecies of doom find an initial appeal only among 'distinguished, individual, pious houses in Jerusalem', who were probably anti-royalist.[6][8] Later, the fulfilment of some of their major political prophecies so impressed the people in Exile that the rational-ethical prophetic message, which was originally the product of marginal men and conditioned by external influences, became incorporated in the heart of the Judeo-Christian tradition. In this way the 'irrational', personal and partly exogenous revolutionary break with existing conditions, epitomised in emissary prophecy, ushers in a new era, and contributes an essential element in the suppression of magic and ritualism, and the growth of methodical-ethical rationalism.

The influence on Weber's outlook of what Mommsen calls 'Nietzche's aristocratic individualism' should not blind us to the fact that for Weber charismatic eruptions and revolutions require, first, appropriate social, economic and, above all, political conditions for their emergence; and second, a collective instrument for their implementation, a party or congregation or community which will continue the leader's work.[6][9] On the other hand, Weber's implicit denial of immanent change or endogenous maturation entailed also a rejection of the Marxist schema which sees social or political revolution as the culmination of a long period of incubation in which latent internal contradictions and conflicts are at last resolved. The revolution may come quite suddenly. The eruption of creative genius, whether in war, politics, religion or art, is certainly bound up with changes in larger groups or 'masses', but stands in a contingent relationship to them both in form and content. Thus the peculiar message of Israelite prophecy cannot be derived from the social conflicts produced by urbanisation, commerce and militarisation. Not even the timing of its appearance is entirely predictable. On the other hand the hero, demagogue or prophet, however much he asserts the value of creative personal liberty, must work with instruments of rationalisation if the revolution he initiates is to bear fruit in the wider community. His charisma, in other words, must be transferred to the organisation of his followers, at the cost of some compromise with pre-existent traditional or legal-rational forms. Hence the problem of revolution is the issue of succession, particularly in modern bureaucratic socieities. Napoleon came to terms with both Vatican and the hereditary principle to ensure continuity;[70] in another way, Lenin succeeded (where Kurt Eisner failed) in moulding the party into an administrative framework for the revolution and not just an instrument of it. 'He who wants to establish absolute justice on earth by force requires a following, a human "machine" .... one of the conditions of success is the depersonalisation and routinisation, in short, the psychic proletarianisation, in the interests of discipline'.[71]

For Weber, then, the sociology of ideology and revolution must set out from the 'meanings' of the participants, and above all from the example and message of the charismatic hero who announces and creates a break with accepted routines. Only in the light of this understanding, do the social circumstances and conflicts in the community, or the resultant organisational processes acquire a significance as necessary elements in the successful revolution. Unlike Marx, for whom the revolution's significance stems from its role as the resolution (and symptom) of underlying long-term contradictions, Weber refuses to understand the heroic movement as an outgrowth of endogenous and structurally determined processes producing malaise or class conflict; there are no determinate sequences or sets of conditions for the appearance of creative ruptures or protests. The drama of conflict between nations and ethnic groups, the continual struggle for power of competing groups embodying opposed values, can change a situation with more or less rapidity, and in such circumstances the prophet or hero and his movement can emerge. The effects of his message and its content are not, however, given by these circumstances.

Irrationality and development

A central theme in the writings of both Marx and Weber is the emancipation of the several domains or sectors of social reality, and the resultant change in their interrelationships. Marx interprets this overall trend within the evolutionist tradition of social growth derived from Western experience. The separation of state and society, of law, theology, politics and art from class structure, neither slackens the dependence, in the long run, of the 'superstructural' elements on the material bases, nor does it threaten the overall reintegration of these separated sectors in the communist society of a socialised humanity. For Weber, on the other hand, the process of disenchantment is both a source of autonomy for the several 'orders', and a means of fragmentation, of subjection of man's creative individuality to the specialised discipline of technical rationality. Weber's understanding of this growth of sectoral autonomy differs profoundly from either the Marxist or the neo-evolutionist approach. For Marx, like the neo-evolutionists, tends to operate with a 'correspondence' model of development; a given level of technology 'corresponds' to a given type of social (class) structure and property relations, and the latter to particular kinds of political and legal systems, and even ideologies and artistic values. So a given state of productive faculties of man requires a 'corresponding form of commerce and consumption', which in turn provide a 'corresponding form of social constitution' and a 'particular political system'.[72] Similarly 'definite forms of social consciousness' correspond with legal and political superstructures, which in turn are based upon definite stages of production and class relations.[73]

It is true that Marx allows a certain latitude for ideology and other modes of consciousness. With reference, for example, to Greek art, Marx acknowledged that 'certain periods of the highest development of art stand in no direct connection to the general development of society, or the material basis and the skeleton structure of its organisation'.[74] He concedes that important artistic forms are possible 'only at an undeveloped stage of art development' and of general social development. Why then do we still enjoy these works, and regard them as artistic models? Because 'the historical childhood of humanity, where it had attained its most beautiful development' exerts the 'eternal charm as an age that will never return', exactly because it sprung from an undeveloped social order.[75]

Ancient Greek art was suffused with mythology which was the 'very ground from which it had sprung', and this accords with Weber's view that religion 'has been an inexhaustible fountain of opportunities for artistic creation, on the one hand, and of stylising through traditionalisation, on the other'.[76] But, whereas Weber goes on to emphasise that intellectualism and rationalisation drive art to become a 'cosmos of more and more consciously grasped independent values which exist in their own right', Marx refuses to concede such an 'irrational' autonomy to a sphere of consciousness. On the contrary: the very individualism of capitalist development intensifies artistic alienation, it isolates the artist from the community, which allows him greater freedom for individual expression, but also threatens formal standards and fundamental human values.[77] Hence social development is always accorded priority as a tool of explanation, the correspondence of aesthetic forms with ideology and social structure is always made clear, even where cultural development *seems* out of step with economic.

In the final analysis, Marx's scheme of social development embodies also a philosophical understanding of the rationality of history. It is in the light of this 'cunning of reason' that

historical changes 'make sense' as the unfolding of the immanent potentialities of man's species-being, his fundamental
human values. No such philosophy of historical rationality
underlies Weber's conceptions. 'Rationalisation' is certainly
an important, even unique, historical trend; so far it has
appeared irresistible. Yet, for Weber, even rationalisation is
subject to historical contingency; even in the West, it has from
time to time receded in the face of determined eruptions by
movements dedicated to an ethic of absolute ends. History
cannot be viewed as a self-enclosed, immanent operation in
which reason and freedom are ultimately vindicated. For
histories, like nations and values, are multiple; the combinations of their relations, the permutations in the value commitments of groups, are too great to allow prediction of the
course of human civilisation as a whole. Finally, history shows
us as much the workings of the 'irrational' and exogenous as
of any predictable internal patterns. Weber even goes so far
as to identify significant change, pattern-breaking movement,
with irrational innovation. It may be, of course, that Weber
was influenced in this by his Protestant background and
nationalist convictions; but his point that ultimately change
derives from the interplay of basically irrational value choices,
brings him to a fundamentally voluntarist and exogenist
standpoint, in which innovation arises from the interaction
and impact of choices made by different groups and spheres
upon each other.

7 Social theory and historical processes

One of the abiding temptations of the study of social change has been the attempt to reduce particular hypotheses to a single, all-encompassing explanation in terms of a prime factor, be it technology or politics or ideas. Where what Moore terms this 'myth of a singular theory of change' has been conceded, the discovery and elaboration of a blanket formula for the derivation of lower-level propositions has proved equally attractive. An example of such a formula would be the 'adaptation' thesis of Steward, or the rival consensus and conflict models advanced in the 1950s. However, as Moore points out, 'None of these determinisms has survived the combined onslaught of logical analysis and opposing facts, and the quest was in any case based on false premises and analogies'.[1] Indeed, similar strictures apply even to more complex bicausal or multifactor approaches, which seek an identical explanation of the whole range of social changes in terms of several variables: either the theory is demonstrably false, or else the variables are of such a general kind as to generate quite vacuous hypotheses for the explanation of specific changes.

Both diffusion*ism* and neo-evolutionism appear to suffer from these defects, if they are regarded as overall theories or frameworks for explaining every kind of social change. Both approaches illuminate important kinds and processes of historical change; yet as general frameworks they are either demonstrably false in the case of diffusion*ism*, or vacuous because they bypass the task of explaining the real mechanisms and sources of change, while adopting a covering formula applicable to every type of change process, as is the case with neo-evolutionism.[2]

Unfortunately, proponents and critics alike have tended to view these approaches as total theories or models of something called 'social change'. In this way, a term for a field of study becomes the designation of a set of phenomena requiring explanation. But, as I have indicated earlier, the processes and forms of social change are so varied and numerous that a significant single theory or framework applicable to all these processes is both undesirable and highly unlikely. Undesirable, because its achievement can only be realised at the cost of the significant differences between different forms and sequences of change; unlikely, because the number of variables involved and their permutations, both in fact and in theory, are so great as to preclude meaningful generalisation. The objects of explanation are, after all, particular sequences of historical changes, whether 'micro-event' process or trendlike sequences, or at most, manageable types of such changes. Even here, there are grave difficulties, as may be witnessed by the elusiveness of a 'theory of modernisation'.[3] Historical types of sequence like conquest, cultural innovation or economic growth, involve a number of variables in varied combinations, which have so far defied wholesale explanations which are not purely vacuous. How much less likely is the discovery of a non-vacuous unitary model of every historical type of change.

There is another reason why a single framework for the explanation of change is likely to prove sterile and inadequate. As we have seen, any theory or model of historical changes, however general or specific, requires a consideration of three issues: the origins and impetus of the change, the channels and mechanisms of its diffusion, and the forms and consequences of the change. Generally speaking, overall theories and models, and even approaches, focus on one or perhaps two of these issues to the relative neglect of the other(s). Even the Marxist and Weberian syntheses emphasise the question of origins and impetus, and devote less attention to questions of channels and forms of change. Such a division of labour introduces the possibility of eclectic combinations in following through a specific kind of change, as in the 'marriages' of diffusion theory with neo-evolutionism, or in anthropological versions of Marxist evolutionism and the Weberian neo-evolutionism of Bellah and Eisenstadt.[4] Given that we are dealing with an extremely broad field of social life, such combinations are only to be expected. Marx himself is eclectic when the occasion demands: his predominantly endogenous account of Western development is dovetailed with a diffusionist theory of non-Western capitalism, for example in India, which in the eyes of some critics, does scant justice to the autochthonous roots of Asian and African economic and political changes.[5]

Endogenous and exogenous models

If there are no convincing overall theories and models of social change, that is because no one underlying approach and image of change can exhaust the rich variety of actual historical sequences. I have drawn attention to two such images, those of flow and continuity and of rupture and intrusion, and have also highlighted the problems for both of the contrast between unintended, unplanned change and the voluntaristic, deliberate kind of change. The resulting categories of 'impact', 'cumulation' and 'selection' do provide a rough-and-ready demarcation and preliminary division of the total field of historical changes; but they fail to do justice to a fourth category of transunit change or interplay of a sustained kind, such as we find in intergroup and interstate relations or in the external relations of key strata.

Whereas the limitations of the voluntaristic category of selection as a master-category for the whole field of social changes are self-evident, in so far as they generally deal with small-scale, short-term event sequences, the limitations of the two macro-approaches and their key categories require a brief recapitulation and extension to bring out the significance of the fourth category, and reveal the legitimacy of a measure of eclecticism.

Neo-evolutionist schemes involve a commitment to an endogenous model of change in a way hardly paralleled by other macro-theories. Such a model represents change as a fairly continuous process of growth and one which realises the immanent potentialities of the unit under consideration. Change, in other words, is a determinate process of development in the sense of both the realisation of potentiality and the subsequent improvement of achievement in successive phases.[6] This is something more than sheer increase of some factor, be it size and scale of population units, number of specialised roles and institutions, or number and complexity of techniques and ideas.

Now, for an understanding of the latter types of change, that is, purely cumulative advances, a neo-evolutionist and endogenous model is both illuminating and apposite. True, some ideas and roles may result from external intrusion and selective response, but on the whole such classical kinds of diffusion influence the *form* of ideas, roles and institutions once these have evolved from within. Thus the voluntary associations which arose in African cities among newly urbanised tribesmen emerged as adaptations to the new demands generated by urban roles and institutions, even where Western democratic ideas and forms played some part in influencing their mode of organisation and procedures.[7] On the other hand, growth models have failed to illuminate the emergence and forms of African millennial movements, which quite clearly owe much to the intrusive quality of European colonialism, as well as to the specific confrontation of traditional religion with Christianity.[8]

As this example shows, the central failing of neo-evolutionism is its inability to take seriously the many radically discontinuous processes and event sequences revealed in the historical record. Categories like strain and malintegration hardly do

125

justice to the considerable incommensurabilities between event sequences before and after external intrusions. The endogenous approach systematically underplays the significance of such intrusive events, neglects the role of chance factors, relegates to the margin of theoretical interest the human response and initiative, and fails to grasp that the manner in which changes occur influences the resultant change.[9] This last factor rules out the possibility of predicting, not merely the rate and intensity of changes, but also their resultant forms. Change is not only rapid today, it is self-propelling, not in the sense of orderly and cumulative growth (though that may also occur), but because a given change process tends to spark off another in a proximate unit or pattern, which then may react back on itself.

For whole ranges and kinds of historical changes, therefore, the neo-evolutionist paradigm and its endogenous model must remain fundamentally irrelevant. It is only in such trendlike changes as increase and decrease (including disintegration) of factors and their consequent interrelations that an endogenous model becomes a useful and necessary tool of analysis.

If the relevance of the endogenous model is seen to be so confined, how shall we view the claims of its rival, the exogenous model of the diffusionists? As we saw, it was necessary to distinguish recent 'diffusion theories' which are mainly descriptive and limited from more thoroughgoing diffusionist approaches, in which the actual mechanism is theoretically less important than the overall approach. Perhaps the most extreme formulation of such exogenism (a better term for such an approach than the rather dated 'diffusionism') can be found in Nisbet's *Social Change and History*. Nisbet holds that most historical change results from the intrusion of an event, which upsets the relatively fixed patterns and habits of society. (He excepts only very small-scale changes, which he thinks frequently cancel themselves out.) Such intrusion always involves a period of conflict and crisis, for men prefer routine and tradition to the discomforts involved in innovation. Change, therefore, is a frequent, but not a normal, occurrence; and persistence is both substantively and methodologically prior to change. Hence when change becomes inevitable men will try to incorporate it as smoothly as possible so as to preserve the identity of their group and its ways as far as they can.[10]

The main strength of such an approach to historical change is that it does answer to our sense of cataclysmic breaks in history, to the observation of frequent and often unexpected ruptures and impacts, which, as it were, break 'open' existing patterns and units. It also accords a central role to intrusive events and event sequences. Given the frequency and effects of wars, trade fluctuations, terrorism, sweeping changes in styles and fashions, the appeal of secular ideologies and the effect of mass media in our century, models of intrusive and exogenous change possess far greater relevance and attraction in the analysis of historical processes today than in earlier eras of more isolated centres and a more fragmented world. Perhaps the only parallels to our heavily internationalised and interrelated era are afforded by the Tell el Amarna age in the mid-second millennium in the Near East and the Hellenistic and Roman epochs, which involved the whole Mediterranean area. In these eras, as today, a diffusion model such as McNeill's, in which change is traced to the balance of power and competition between rival economic and cultural centres, is far more apposite than the standard endogenous accounts of immanent change, which take the 'society' as the terminal unit of analysis.[11]

Intrusion models, it should be added, are not confined solely to the case of relations between states and cultures. Patterns of activity, embodied often in institutions, are also amenable to this kind of analysis. A change in educational policy or methods may on occasion be traced to the (competitive) influence of external ideas and models, even though it is mediated by various interest groups in a particular society. Equally, educational or religious changes may result from the

127

impact of changes in other 'regions' within the society or culture, for example the economic or political sphere; and conversely, as Weber demonstrated, economic change can be heavily influenced by changes occurring in the religious sector. Even such sheltered institutions as the family may experience the impact of massive shifts in other institutional areas, as Smelser documented in his study of the British working-class family during the Industrial Revolution in Lancashire.[1][2] Nor is the family immune to sudden intrusive change from units far removed in culture and geography: witness the dramatic effect on West European family budgets and life-styles of oil price increases and wars fought outside Europe.

Even on a subject like revolution, traditionally the domain of endogenous models, the greater relevance and power of exogenous models of intrusion becomes increasingly evident today. The usual Western model of social and political revolution, which stems from the French example, is becoming increasingly obsolete in the study of non-Western revolutions. To see revolutions in Africa, Asia and even Latin America as symptoms or cures of a long internal disease, as Brinton did with the four 'classical' revolutions of America, England, France and Russia, fails to capture the underlying influences at work outside Europe.[1][3] So, on the whole, does the traditional Marxist analysis of class contradictions. For as Marx himself realised, what stands out about modern revolutions is the impact of external event sequences (colonial, mercantile, missionary) on their genesis and forms. Granted that every society displays a measure of tension between groups, norms and institutions, the problem is to understand why there was a revolutionary solution or route, and why it occurred where and when it did. In the case of more recent revolutions the answer to such questions must start from an interstate and interinstitutional context of group conflict, and from the impact of external ideas, techniques and power complexes acting as referents, models or coercive agents on elites and other strata within a given unit. Even the classical revolutions of France and Russia require a perspective which accords more weight than traditional models allow, to the impact of foreign powers and transnational movements of trade, ideas, techniques and personnel on the origins as well as the timing and form of the ensuing revolutions.[14]

'Interplay' and transunit change

Despite its greater historical relevance and power, the exogenous model suffers from a number of drawbacks if it is applied in too undiscriminating a manner. To begin with, it tends to assume that all change is qualitative and thus overlooks the role of quantitative changes of size, scale and frequency. Of course, such quantitative movements may not of themselves indicate a significant change, nor need they entail it, a point that much neo-evolutionist thought underrates. However, even purely quantitative increases or decreases may produce modifications or even replacements of given patterns or units, as when a 'patrimonial' bureaucracy gradually changes towards the 'rational-legal' type through the proliferation of new tasks and offices, or massive urbanisation changes the character of a town. In both cases a cumulative succession of events led to significant changes in existing patterns or units; and exogenous models tend to overlook such important sequences.

They also tend to neglect the role of active 'selection' by individuals and groups, a problem I raised at the end of chapter 5. There I argued that the sort of ideological diffusionism exemplified by Kedourie and Nisbet in their different ways, underrates the creative responses of men and women threatened or tempted by external pressures or opportunities. So, for example, the way in which the two world wars affected attitudes and institutions in the combatant countries was, in part, a function of the existing traditions and perceptions, and of the resourcefulness and adaptability of different

129

groups sharing specific values and ideals. Similarly with the impact of contemporary events like inflation and terrorism: its effects are being continually mediated by variations in planned responses to crises, and by creative initiatives of strongly motivated individuals and groups, factors which an exogenous model again fails to incorporate.

Third, exogenism fails to provide criteria for isolating the kinds of external historical event sequences which are likely to produce significant change. Strictly speaking, any intrusion by external event sequences modifies in some degree existing patterns; but the real questions, in practice, concern, first, the kind and degree of change which can be termed 'significant', and second, the type and intensity of external event chains deemed likely to induce such change. So, for example, we necessarily distinguish the effects of economic recessions from those produced by changes in fashions, but do so for reasons quite extraneous to the assumptions and tenets of exogenism. Matters are less simple when we try to assess the relative 'significance' of the effects of economic depressions or wars as against changes in styles such as Romanticism in music and literature or Impressionism in the visual arts, since the latter constitute revolutions in our sensibilities, subtly working themselves into the wider social consciousness, even affecting several generations after the events, just as much as any social or political revolution induced by wars and recessions. Here, then, we are forced back on to a Weberian position in the choice of what constitutes significant change, independent of the exogenous/endogenous debate. As for the criteria of 'significant impact', this is a largely unexplored field, which awaits comparative studies to assess the relative weight of different kinds of external event sequences.

Such research leads inevitably into an area of change, which the exogenous model (in this respect, like its endogenous rival) overlooks or misrepresents. This is the transnational or more broadly 'transunit' type of change, which I briefly mentioned, and which I called, for want of a better term, 'inter-

130

play' or 'interaction' between patterns and units. Much change is the product of mutual interactions between neighbouring, or even distant, sectors or units which may stand in varying relationships over some decades or generations. This sort of change is ignored by exogenists who always treat event sequences as *in*trusive. Events never originate from the unit under consideration; nor does exogenism allow for a two-way interaction between a unit and its 'partners'. (The same strictures apply, *mutatis mutandis*, to their account of relations between patterns like activities and institutions.) This one-sided account of change processes stems, in part, from the assumption that units can and must be clearly delimited, over against their environment (including other units). Curiously, exogenists treat units as hermetic systems almost as much as their neo-evolutionist counterparts—an assumption which makes sense in a world of zealously sovereign nation-states, perhaps, but runs into difficulties both analytical and historical (consider the controversies over Marx's delimitation of an 'economic' sphere, or over Wittfogel's contrast of 'feudal' and 'oriental despotic' structures.)[1 5]

Quite apart from these difficulties, it is possible to ignore a rigid distinction between immanentist and exogenist principles and models of change, and opt for a stance of theoretical indifference which Martins has termed an *isogenous* mode of explanation.[1 6] As Martins points out, in much theoretical work there is no need to stress the endogenous/exogenous dichotomy. In the field of historical changes, however, the issue remains fundamental for practical as well as theoretical reasons. Practically, we often need to locate the origins and course of specific changes so as to be able to furnish suitable responses; and similarly with our need to grasp the mechanisms of diffusion so as to encourage or impede innovations or adaptations. On a more theoretical plane, it is important to understand the difference in various kinds of change between mere catalysts and precipitants or accelerators of change, and real impact and intrusion, which form the core of causal event sequences inducing significant transformations, irrespective of the previous states of the unit or pattern. The endogenous/exogenous dichotomy also provides a useful criterion for classifying various event sequences, and a referent against which man's creative initiatives can be measured. In actual historical work, dealing with specific micro-events and processes, the distinction is indispensable, and in practice we do know how to demarcate patterns and units, albeit only approximately and with varying degrees of agreement.

This leaves intact the criticism that exogenism treats the unit too hermetically, and assumes too great a cleavage between unit and environment. This is where the fourth category of changes, the transunit interactions, provides a necessary foil and complement to that of 'intrusion'. As I said, such long-term, more or less continuous patterns of interplay and 'partnership' between two or more patterns or units can come, in time, to provide a source and context for changes within particular units within that constellation. Change in this case proceeds between and across units and patterns, and results from the convergence and interplay of event sequences which link the partners in a given nexus of centres. So, for example, the linkages and rivalries between the concert of European states in the age of absolutism provided a source and theatre for the rise of new movements like the Enlightenment or nationalism, which in turn affected all the units within that constellation.[16]

Types of transunit or interactive changes range from the technological and economic to religious and artistic developments. Examples include the decline of cities and states as a result of changes in trade routes and the discovery of new markets, as in the case of Genoa and Venice; the birth of syncretic cults consequent on the interaction of Hellenism with Near Eastern religious cultures; the origins of recent wars in the context of ethnic and national antagonisms and interstate economic competition; scientific and intellectual discoveries stemming from cosmopolitan exchanges between scholars, as well as from the close relations between intellectual and other spheres; the changing relationships between patrons and artistic traditions which pave the way for stylistic innovations, or between rival centres which facilitate the rise of new styles such as Mannerism or neo-classicism; or the much-studied examples of interethnic and interstate relationships in the rise and breakdown of empires like Rome or Tsarist Russia.

In these and other cases the basic precept in the analysis of transunit changes involves the tracing of its origin and course to the pattern of interactions between a given unit and others surrounding it. If some cumulative changes can be traced to the workings of factors within a given pattern or unit, there remain some broad changes whose origin and development must be sought in a wider context of relationships between that unit and its partners. Where changes cannot be convincingly ascribed to either cumulation or sudden intrusion, or to voluntaristic planning, there is a prima facie case for deriving them from the linkages and currents formed by a given unit with others with whom it stands in mutually interinfluencing relations. Only empirical analysis can reveal how much of the change can be so derived; but it can safely be claimed that a large part of the historical record would be incomprehensible without explanations in terms of transunit influences. In a sense, much of history can be usefully interpreted in terms of such interactions, with units and whole areas oscillating between epochs of extreme dialogue and interpenetration, and of relative isolation and withdrawal. Synoecism and fragmentation form basic poles in social experience, and it is possible to interpret a fair portion of cultural changes in a given era in terms of such oscillations, as has been done with the succession of cultures in the ancient Near East from the Mesolithic era to the early dynasties in Sumer and Egypt.[17] Periods of continuous and productive contact alternate with eras of isolation and boundary erection; amalgamations and fusions are succeeded by tendencies to disintegration and atomisation, in which a low level of interunit linkage profoundly affects the rate and course of subsequent change.

Of course, such oscillating movements have often been discerned, but the attention of historians and others has usually been focused on the conditions of such fusions and disintegrations rather than their consequences for subsequent changes. Here the point is that interpenetration or close relations, or conversely weak linkages, themselves constitute basic conditions of changes within the constituent units. Thus in the field of cultural change it is possible to trace the formation of new styles to the nexus of mutual influences between different cultural centres. Thus the rise of the Florentine Renaissance style in the painting of Masaccio and Lippi or the sculpture of Donatello can be traced back to the confluence and interaction of several factors stemming from different sectors and units, from the new humanism of religious orders like the Franciscans and Dominicans with their different artistic needs, from the novelties of the Burgundian International Gothic court art, from the literary, and then artistic, rediscovery of classical antiquity and of Roman monuments—all interacting with the native Giottesque tradition whose course had been interrupted by the crisis of the Black Death.[18] Similarly, Rousseau's cult of nature mingled with the impact of excavations at Herculaneum and Pompei and the influence of Shaftesbury's philosophy of sentiment, also exemplified in the English novel, to create a new set of links between England, France and Rome which bred the revolutionary neo-classical movement in art, literature and finally politics.[19]

In the field of modern social movements, too, an 'interactive' model becomes indispensable. The limitations of purely endogenous models must by now be apparent. Strictly, exogenous models also tend towards a superficial diffusionism, which, as we saw, ignores the important contributions stemming from a unit's traditions, and the values of its members. It is interesting that there is usually a considerable interval between the first impact of colonial intrusion into a given area and the rise of native nationalist or socialist movements. In this interval the external unit of domination (or dominant influence, as the case may be) and the subject area become involved in a definite set of relations which, if not symmetrical, are never only one-way, as the diffusionists would maintain. Even outright possession of a territory exerts an influence back upon the occupying power, whose classes and strata change their forms of struggle in the light of the new external situation. Moreover, it is the exact form of relationship between dominating power and subject people, the instruments of suppression, the conflict between their cultures and ideals, which act as sources and repertoires for the form and content of subsequent nationalist or communist movements. Thus the fact that 'scientific' bureaucracy, requiring a trained intelligentsia to man it, was the pre-eminent agent of European rule, constituted a major factor in the rise and nature of subsequent nationalisms.[20]

Analysis of change in terms of transunit interactions presupposes a world of rival power centres, which exert mutual influences of a nature which is often quite different from that intended by their elites and ruling classes. How these power centres are formed and decline, how new centres of influence take their place, are subjects that form the core of a truly historical sociology, along with the cultural changes that they initiate and which in turn influence political action. It is an area of change which, though long familiar to historians engaged in unravelling event sequences in specific areas or units, has only sporadically engaged the attention of sociologists. All that can be done here is to reaffirm the need for a structural historical sociology, which differs from that usually envisaged under that heading by placing transunit influences, mutual interactions between rival centres of power and culture, at the heart of the sociology of historical change.

Conclusion: the creative response

It is within such a structural context of transunit influences that planned changes and creative responses, so important a part of contemporary change, take place. Put differently, an 'action frame of reference' such as Banks and others derive from Weber, operates within a much broader structural context than that usually envisaged by structuralists who think in terms of largely immanent change and endogenous models. But exactly that breadth of context allows far greater room for human ingenuity and initiative. In fact, the greater the exposure of a given unit or pattern to influences from other units, the greater the likelihood of variations in response to changing situations, whether cumulative or intrusive in origin. The response to a given situation is never wholly given in the logic of that situation, partly because of the complexity of situations which derive from the confluence of many chains emanating from different units, and partly because of an irrational element stemming from distinctive value commitments of those who, at a given moment, are able to direct affairs or guide the community's response to changing situations. The most obvious example of this irrationality is the creativity of genius. Thus in the example of Florentine Renaissance art above, the peculiar forms and content of that innovatory style cannot be simply derived from the confluence of trends which I enumerated; they arise also from the creative synthesis and reworking of received sources by the artist, in the light of his personal vision and of the ideals of his circle and patrons. Similarly, with founders of new sects or religions: Pauline Christianity, though much of its doctrine and symbolism can be derived from the interactive influence of gnostic and neo-platonic thought with Jewish ethics and beliefs, and these in turn with the exigencies of the Pax Romana, nevertheless could not have evolved as it did without the distinctive stamp of value commitment and beliefs of the founders as they wrestled with a spiritual and political crisis in the first century Near East.[2][1]

It follows then that an exogenous or interactive model, because of its greater 'openness', must allow an important, but not overriding, role for individual and group creativity in the shaping of changes. Individual charisma and group ideals and organisation mediate the impact of event sequences from external sources, and filter the influences that stem from links between rival centres. Weber's emphasis on such 'irrational' elements receives a stronger impetus from the very variety of combinations of influences, while conversely that variety of permutations evokes a far greater role for human responses and creative 'selection', as it emerges from rival 'images of the world' held by warring groups and factions. Similarly, the wider context of an exogenous or interactive approach to change gives greater prominence to the mutual 'fit' between images of the world and their social bearers, which Weber discussed through his concept of 'elective affinity'. Given this strong external referent, various classes and status groups may now select ideologies and conceptions which originate either in other, often distant, units, or in the interactions of 'their' unit with its partners; conversely, ideas and movements which find little response in the units of their pioneering, may well seek social carriers elsewhere, who can mould these conceptions to fit their own interests and power position. In a way, then, exogenous or transunit interaction models of change take Weber's conceptions a stage further than he envisaged, both as regards the relation between ideas and their bearers and in relation to the creative role of groups and individuals. Such models also reinforce Weber's insistence on the struggle of competing political and cultural centres, making this structural element the starting-point and context of a sociology of change.

Beyond these general considerations it is also clear that the analysis of transunit influence must pay considerable attention to the more subtle cultural movements, which colour and guide the conceptions of leaders and other groups within given units. This is where the images of intellectuals and intelligentsias play a vital role. Without going so far as Nomad and Kautsky in claiming that modern secular movements are largely the handiwork of the intellectuals, their role as *mediators* of change, and particularly of the forms that change takes, can hardly be overestimated. Indeed, the familiar combination of ideas, movements and intellectuals (and intellectualisation) has shaped the course of many movements in pre-modern eras of change, even where specific interests and geo-political limitations have provided the impetus and framework of subsequent changes.[22] This is partly because intellectual strata have greater access to the motives and conceptions, not only of their counterparts in other units, but also of the influential elites abroad. Hence they act as sensitisers and conductors of interunit influences, just as wandering minorities in the medieval world became carriers and interpreters of different cultural traditions between even fairly isolated civilisations and states.

In emphasising the importance of transunit interactions, I do not wish to appear to dismiss the validity and utility of other models of change, whether of the traditional endogenous variety or the more recent exogenous type, provided always that they confine their attention to those event sequences which they are well-equipped to handle. So varied are the types of change, that it will always be possible and legitimate to select some processes and trends which are peculiarly amenable to analysis and illumination by either endogenous or exogenous models. The argument here has concerned the importance in the historical record, not only of sudden cataclysmic intrusions, but of broader and more lasting interactions between patterns and units, which form the essential setting for analyses of human responses and innovations in the light of unique value commitments and ideals. It is in this dialogue between, on the one hand, the ever-changing context and web of interunit relations, and, on the other, creative human syntheses and initiatives, that much significant change—its origins, mechanisms and forms— can be located and understood.

References and further reading

Details of books and articles to which reference is made are given in the Bibliography which follows.

Chapter 1 The nature of change

1. Cf. Hillier (1968) on such revivals in Britain.
2. Cf. Gouldner (1959).
3. For some historians' views on the proximity of history and sociology (and for the converse argument that history is a generalising discipline) cf. Carr (1961), pp.62-7 and Plumb (1969), pp.84-5, 114.
4. Nisbet (1969), pp.271-2.
5. For the durability of caste in India, cf. Dumont (1970). On feudal estates in Europe and Japan, cf. Coulborn ed. (1956).
6. Moore (1963), p.2.
7. This is forcefully argued by Gusfield (1967) among others.
8. For the endurance of basic forms or styles in such matters as dress and cuisine both in the East and West, cf. Kroeber (1963), ch. 1.
9. Cf. Also the distinction between genetic and classificatory variation in Nisbet (1969), pp.194-8.
10. On the chronological range and variety of empires, cf. Eisenstadt (1963); on the differences between modern revolutions, cf. Leiden and Schmitt (1968), and Johnson (1964).
11. Nisbet (1969), p.168.
12. Pareto did envisage some lasting changes in the economic and ideological spheres, for example secularisation, but held that such changes did not affect the basic cyclical

pattern of elite rule during the course of Western history; cf. Finer, ed. (1966).

13. For other examples of such breakdowns and replacements, cf. Kann (1950) on the collapse of the Habsburg empire. An equally important type of sequence is the amalgamation of several small units in a single large one, which greatly modifies their distinctive character, as happened in Germany and to a lesser extent in Italy, cf. Holborn (1964), and Beales (1971).

Chapter 2 Varieties of change

1. Radcliffe-Brown (1957), esp. pp.71-89.
2. This question is critically examined by Cancian (1960).
3. For an excellent discussion of date-classes and plural times, cf. Martins (1974), esp. pp. 264-9.
4. Braudel (1969).
5. Cf. Buckley (1967) for this cybernetic formulation.
6. For prehistoric trends, cf. Clark and Piggott (1965). For geosocial trends uncovered by archaeology in later periods, cf. Collins *et al.* (1970). Geosocial or geohistorical trends may also refer to the rhythms of interaction between populations and their environments during recorded history, which provide an essential setting for processes and micro-events.
7. One can distinguish between a sociological history which tends to be more period—or country-oriented (as with Rude's or Lefebvre's work on the French Revolution, Bloch's (1965) study of feudal society in Europe and Pye's (1962) analysis of Burmese politics), and 'historical sociology' which focuses on problems and concepts, such as Wittfogel's (1957) study, *Oriental Despotism* or Barrington-Moore's (1967) analysis of agrarian origins of democracy and dictatorship. An 'interunitary' approach, stressing relationships between states and ethnic groups and regions, will lay more stress on the order of events

and the time context in which specific empires, revolutions or dictatorships emerge. So, for example, there are considerable differences in type between the early empires of the Near East and China, and the later ones of Rome, Byzantium, Islam and Russia, whose increased complexity is partly a function of their position in time and in tradition. The importance of received traditions (involving memories of earlier relationships) is another reason for retaining an overall chronological baseline for 'general' history.

8. On the Baroque, cf. Friedrich (1952) and Wittkower (1973).

9. It is possible, but hardly worth while, to separate the 'social' from the 'economic' dimension. In practice the two dimensions are inextricably linked. What is illegitimate is the enlargement of the economic dimensions to touch on every other element. This was one of Weber's criticisms of the Marxist use of the 'economic' factor in historical explanations, resulting from a failure to distinguish analytically between the strictly economic and the 'economically conditioned' and 'economically relevant', cf. Aron (1967), pp.238-9.

10. Cf. Lenski (1966). But Eisenstadt (1963) suggests some tensions between rulers and military commanders in empires.

11. On political intelligentsias and radical change in Africa and Asia today, cf. Kautsky, ed. (1962) and Shils (1962).

12. A broad definition of culture in terms of the 'distinctive way of life of a group of people', including both tangible and intangible creations is given in Kluckhohn (1951), and Kroeber (1952).

13. Kroeber (1963), ch. 2, especially pp. 26,32-7, which rather overestimates the 'developmental flow' (like the 'trajectory of a missile', p.35) of a given style, at the cost of impacts from other sectors and from other units.

14. Cf. Cobban (1965) and Rude (1963).

15. On the aims of early British governors of India, cf. McCulley (1966).
16. On the Orthodoxy of the Jerusalem Christians under James and Peter, and the consequences of their disappearance in 70, cf. Brandon (1967), and Carmichael (1966).
17. Cf. Goldthorpe, Lockwood *et al.* (1968).
18. On Alexander's aims, cf. Burn (1973), who sets those aims in the context of a general Greek drive to the East, chs. 2,15.
19. Cf. Bordes (1968).
20. The importance of specific natural disasters, coming at 'crucial moments', such as the plague that carried off Pericles in Attica at the start of the Peloponnesian War, is sometimes overlooked. But such chance factors need not be viewed only as precipitants or accelerators; they also function as contexts and conditions for subsequent event sequences of human decisions, depending on the interpretation of their role by the participants for their full effects.

Chapter 3   Images of change

1. Cf. Moore (1963), pp.33-44 for a sophisticated discussion of these cumulative theories of the direction of change.
2. Lerner (1958), ch.2.
3. Lenski (1966), ch.4, esp. pp.90-3.
4. Cf. Gellner (1964), ch.2, esp. p.45.
5. Finer, ed. (1966), Pt. I.ii/3-4, Pt. II, ii/4, iii/3-5, and Introduction pp.51-71.
6. Psalm 103; 15-16.
7. *Iliad* VI, 146-9.
8. O. Spengler *The Decline of the West* (1926), cited in Kroeber (1963), ch.4.
9. N. Danilevsky: *Russia and Europe* (1871), cited in Kroeber (1963), ch.5.

10. Toynbee (1954).
11. Nisbet (1969) and (1970a), Pt. II; also Bock (1963).
12. Durkheim (1947b), p.3; on Durkheim's evolutionism, cf. Fletcher (1974), and Bellah (1959).
13. Rostow (1960).
14. For early British and Scottish evolutionism, cf. Burrow (1966).
15. For holism, cumulation and immanentism, cf. van den Berghe (1963) and Ginsberg (1957), especially chs.10, 12.
16. Cf. Bock (1964).
17. Spencer (1900).
18. Cf. Spencer's *Principles of Sociology* (1876) for his social classifications.
19. L. Morgan, *Ancient Society* (1877), cited in Nisbet (1969), pp.159-60.
20. J.F. McLennan: *Studies in Ancient History*, 2nd series (1896), cited in Burrow (1966), pp.12-13.
21. E.B. Tylor (1889), cited in Nisbet (1969).
22. Tylor (1881), cited in Nisbet (1969), p.199.
23. Comte (1896), II, 249, though he remained committed to the method of conjectural history.
24. Spencer (1896), II, 331.
25. As with Comte's 'law of three stages', or Marx's 'economic law of motion of modern society'.
26. Cf. Comte's interest in 'abstract history' free of distortions generated by exceptional events.
27. Cf. Carr's comments on I. Berlin, *Historical Inevitability*, 1954, in Carr (1964), pp.91-108.
28. Cf. Frank (1969), and Shils (1961).
29. Martins (1974), pp.280-1.
30. Cf. Daniel (1971), and Lowie (1938), ch.10, for a critique of hyperdiffusionism.
31. By Garrod and Clark (1967).
32. Cf. Childe (1936) and (1942); but cf. his later *Social Evolution* (1951).
33. Cf. Harris (1968), and Heine-Geldern (1956).

34. Elliot Smith (1932); cf. the criticisms in Boas (1924).
35. Cf. Lowie (1938); and Daniel (1971), pp.103-5 on 'stimulus diffusion'.

Chapter 4   Neo-evolutionism

1. Sahlins and Service (1960).
2. White (1949).
3. Steward (1955), and (1960) pp.169-86.
4. Cf. the discussion in Wertheim (1974), pp.37-8, 54-7, citing C. Geertz, *Agricultural Involution: the processes of ecological change in Indonesia*, 1963.
5. Coulborn (1959) ch.5, citing in support Frankfort (1948) and (1956).
6. Daniel (1971), pp.89-94, 103-5. Cultural borrowing was much more limited in the case of Shang China, pp.123-5. In general, however, cultural diffusion increases with time, further limiting the utility of an adaptation thesis.
7. Cf. the remarks on Sorokin and Toynbee in Boskoff (1964), and on Danilevsky, Spengler, Toynbee, Sorokin and Coulborn, in Kroeber (1963), chs. 4-5 and Appendices.
8. Moore (1963), pp.75-6.
9. Durkheim (1947a) and Gouldner (1962).
10. The most succinct statement of the position by a neo-evolutionist is Parsons (1961). Cf. also Eisenstadt (1970) for a rather different general account, and Smith (1937b), ch.2.
11. Bellah (1964).
12. Parsons (1966).
13. For the term 'cladogenesis', cf. Dobzhansky (1962) p.190: 'The evolution of the animal kingdom . . . is usually represented as a branching tree. . . . The tree thus symbolises the *cladogenesis* . . . , i.e. the adaptive radiation, the tendency of the evolutionary stream to become subdivided into numerous branches, only to have most of them become extinct because of failures to keep adjusted to changing environments.'

14. For a fuller exposition of this critique of the concept of differentiation, cf. Smith (1973b), chs.3, 6.
15. Cf. Noth (1960), and Kaufmann (1961), especially ch 4 on the cultic expression of Israelite religion and its popular basis.
16. In a sense differentiation is one of these pattern-variables as the opposite of a functionally diffuse orientation. But differentiation also subsumes all the pattern variables marking the most generalised historical trend from the 'traditional' half of each pair to the 'modern' and special ised, cf. Parsons (1964).
17. This ethnocentrism appears, for example, in Parsons's article on 'evolutionary universals', (Parsons, 1964): cf also Hoselitz (1960).
18. Parsons (1971).
19. Bellah (1958) and (1965), esp. the Epilogue.
20. Bellah (1965) and (1963).
21. Weber does, however, emphasise the tensions between religion and various 'orders', or sectors, of the world (family, economic, political, aesthetic, erotic and intellectual) whose 'internal and lawful autonomy' religious rationalisation accentuates and makes conscious; but again these 'individual spheres' are a product of a specific trend of rationalisation, which is largely occidental. The consequence does, of course, *condition* subsequent development; but nowhere does Weber single out this consequence as the criterion of a social typology, let alone as an active cause of change. Cf. Weber, ed. 'Religious rejections of the World and their directions', in Gerth and Mill (1948).
22. T. Parsons, Introduction to Weber (1966).
23. Eisenstadt (1973), p.209. The other vital factor was the combination of these assumptions with 'the development of far-reaching structural-organisational changes, especially in the economic and political fields', and were spread throughout the world by protest movements able to create new centres for expansion (*ibid.*).

24. Eisenstadt (1973), pp.217-8, citing Luethy (1964), 26-38, and Luethy, *La Banque Protestante en France*, Paris SEVPEN, 2 vols. 1959-61.
25. *Ibid.*, p.140.
26. *Ibid.*, p.226. Protestantism's transformative performance was most far-reaching where the Protestant groups were 'secondary elites', 'close to but not identified with central elites', as in Holland.
27. *Ibid.*, pp.217, 222-4. But such new and fairly secularised bases were already present in Machiavelli's Italy, only to be crushed by the armies of Charles V and Spain.
28. Cf. Hay (1961).
29. Honour (1968) and Rosenblum (1967).
30. Levy (1966), Pts. I and IV, ch.2.
31. Eisenstadt (1973), p.259: 'By and large, modernity was an indigenous development in Western Europe, whereas its spread to Central and Eastern Europe and beyond to Asia, Africa and to some extent, also Latin America, was the result of external forces impinging on traditional societies and civilisation'.
32. Apter (1965) and (1968).
33. Cf. Almond (1960).
34. Eisenstadt (1973) ch.12, esp. pp.270-80; cf. Levy (1953).
35. In Smelser (1968), see 'Towards a theory of modernisation'.
36. Smelser (1959), esp. pp.32 ff. for his seven stage sequence.
37. Smelser (1968) 'Towards a general theory of social change'. In the essays in this collection, Smelser allows a greater role to the intervening psychological variables.
38. On differential transformative capacities among Third World states, cf. Eisenstadt (1964b) and (1968b). The argument resembles the Hegelian theory of 'historyless peoples' (i.e. state-building nations were true or 'great' nations, but 'nations' which had to date not built states, were inherently incapable of doing so,—and hence were doomed specimens . . 'ethnographic monuments').

39. Smelser (1962), esp. chs.1, 9.
40. *Ibid.*, ch.10; Geertz's critique in Apter (1963).
41. Cf. also Smelser (1968), pp.97-100.
42. For a much fuller discussion of the neo-evolutionist treatment of social movements and revolutions, cf. Smith (1973b) ch.5.
43. Johnson (1968).
44. For such elite strategies and 'precipitants', cf. Eckstein (1964).
45. This point is emphasised in the excellent critique of such schemes in Stone (1966). Overdetermination also figures, though differently, in Kornhauser's urban anomie thesis, cf. Kornhauser (1959) and Gusfield (1962).
46. Eisenstadt (1964b).
47. Cf. the distinctions outlined in Eisenstadt (1965).
48. Deutsch (1961).
49. Cf. the plea in Homans (1964).
50. On the neo-evolutionist tendency to reduce external elements to the status of theoretical adjuncts, by correlating their endogenist bias with an 'accidentalist' view of events, cf. Smith (1937b) esp. ch.7.

Chapter 5   Diffusion

1. Thomas and Znaniecki (1927).
2. Cf. Park (1915) and the discussion of Park in Boskoff (1964).
3. Cf. Nettl and Robertson (1968), esp. Pt. II, for the introduction of communication systems by Third World elites and their use as an index of 'modernisation', independent of economic development and industrialisation.
4. Cf. Wilkinson (1974).
5. See for example Lagos (1963) and Horowitz (1966).
6. E.K. Scheuch, 'Cross-national comparisons with aggregate data', in Merritt and Rokkan, eds. (1966).

7. A point made cogently by M. Guessous, 'A general critique of equilibrium theory', in Moore and Cook, eds. (1967).
8. Cf. Smith (1975) for a discussion of the differences be- tween classical diffusionism and recent 'micro-diffusion'.
9. Deutsch (1966), esp. ch.4.
10. *Ibid.*, ch.7, p.162.
11. *Ibid.*, ch.6, for the relation between mobilisation and as- similation.
12. Lerner (1958) esp. ch.2.
13. *Ibid.*, p.55.
14. *Ibid.*, pp.49-51.
15. *Ibid.*, ch.1, esp. pp.23-5, for attitudes in the village of Balgat, near Ankara (now a suburb).
16. Pye (1962), p.38.
17. *Ibid.*, p.53. Pye sees the process of 'national building' as a response to international forces, especially to the diffusion of a new 'world culture based upon modern science and technology', modern practices of organisation, and modern standards of governmental performance', pp.10-14.
18. Cf. also Binder (1964) and Halpern (1963).
19. Cf. Almond and Pye, eds. (1965), and Pye and Verba (1965).
20. Deutsch (1966). He also thinks mass emigrations are de- clining.
21. Tylor (1865). 'Diffusion' and 'invention' were regarded as processes of change, not explanatory principles, by evolu- tionists.
22. Rogers (1962), p.19.
23. *Ibid.*, p.13: cf. also 'Adoption is a decision to continue full use of the innovation', p.17, while 'an innovation is an idea perceived as new by the individual', p.13.
24. Cf. Tarde (1903), as cited by Rogers.
25. Rogers (1962), pp.301-4.
26. Cf. Park (1950).
27. Hagen (1962). Hagen operates, not with 'typical' actors, but through personality types—the conservative peasant,

the innovative entrepreneur, the authoritarian father, etc.,— and the decisive mechanism remains psychological: the 'retreatism' of disparaged groups, and the consequent need to vent aggression within the family, which later produces creative sons. All this, despite his own caveat that 'sequences of action and reaction within individuals are difficult to analyse', p.201.

28. McClelland (1960) and idem: 'The achievement motive in economic growth', in Hoselitz and Moore eds. (1963).

29. Cf. the criticisms in Kunkel (1965).

30. LaPiere (1965), p.39.

31. *Ibid.*, esp. ch.6.

32. For LaPiere (*ibid.*, p.30) the 'essential problem of social change' is 'how various new elements come into being and gain acceptance in the society of their origin', 'Socially significant change' is defined as a new thing adopted by many people and integrated into the social system, so that it endures for more than a generation (as opposed to fads and fashions).

33. Cf. Palmer (1959) and Godechot (1965) for the 'Atlantic' thesis of the Revolution. Rude (1963) sets the French Revolution in its European context, but emphasises its unique features in relation to other national-democratic movements.

34. Nolte (1965); Kornhauser (1959); cf. the fine balance between 'European' and 'German' features, and long-range trends and short-range processes and events, maintained by Bracher (1973).

35. Trevor-Roper (1961). His 'secondary' cases include Czechs and Slovaks, Serbs, Poles, Ukrainians, Romanians and Jews.

36. *Ibid.*, p.11. The new nationalism 'was not episodic, nor the mere result of temporary circumstances, like the periodic outbursts of the past. It was a new general idea, powerful, even irresistible, as new ideas can be; and it rendered all old politics useless, old remedies unavailing',

(pp.16-17). Trevor-Roper does not, however, expand on the change in circumstances at which he hints here, and which lend the new idea such power and appeal.

37. Kedourie (1960); for a fuller discussion of Kedourie's thesis, cf. Smith (1971), chs.1-2.

38. Kedourie (1971), Introduction, expands his ideological diffusionist thesis to African and Asian elites, with a wealth of examples. Cf. the comments and an alternative explanation in Smith (1973a).

39. Kedourie (1960), pp.99, 105, for the 'need to belong' and the 'spirit of the age'.

40. Teggart (1925).

41. Cf. Kautsky, ed. (1962) Introduction, for such adaptations in Russia and China.

42. Cf. the criticisms of facile psychologistic diffusionism in T. Hodgkin; 'The relevance of "Western" ideas in the derivation of African nationalism', in Pennock (1964).

43. The term is Kohn's—cf. H. Kohn (1967), esp. pp.16-19.

44. Banks (1972).

45. Cf. Coleman *et al.* (1966).

46. Banks (1972) p.25. In contrast to the vague aspirations and unrealistic activism of millenarian movements in the Middle Ages, 'self-help' movements like the Co-operatives or socialism were realistic and practical, and concerned with how exactly to implement their ideals in society.

47. *Ibid.*, p.23.

48. *Ibid.*, pp.13-16, 35-6.

49. Heberle (1951); Banks (1972), p.31, citing S.C. Gilfillan; *The Sociology of Invention*, MIT Press, 1970.

50. Wilkinson (1971), p.104. The full definition, with discussion, is elaborated on pp.26-9.

51. *Ibid.*, pp.151-4.; Banks (1972), p.13, and ch.4.

52. Banks (1972), p.33; cf. also p.13.

53. *Ibid.*, pp.41 sqq.

54. *Ibid.*, pp.39-40. Ideology, despite its many adaptations to situational exigencies, is also moulded by underlying

'images of the world', fundamental standpoints vis-a-vis the world, which shape its 'advocational rhetoric' as much as organisational needs of the moment. The vision shapes the movement, even after it has created it; it continues to define the movement, even though it comes to mean different things to different people and groups at different times and places. This allows us to make at least some generalisations about, say, communism, nationalism and even fascism.

55. For the role of social comparisons in generating revolutionary dissent, cf. Urry (1973), esp. Pt. II.

Chapter 6   Marx and Weber

1. Marx and Engels (1947), p.19.
2. That which makes man's life distinct from the existence of animals is social production, the quality of being *homo faber*, a socially creative being, who, for example, has humanised desires and a sense of beauty, and considers himself to be a 'universal and consequently free being', cf. *Economic and Philosophic Manuscripts* (1844), in Easton and Guddat, eds. (1967).
3. Cf. the criticism of Feuerbach's anthropology for its ahistorical character in the *Theses on Feuerbach* (1845), and the tentative historical scheme of property forms in the first part of *The German Ideology* (1846), the first clear statements of Marx's 'historical materialism'. One of Marx's central points is that man's needs are not fixed like the animals', but changing and increasing through man's own activities in order to cope with his existing set of needs at any given moment in time: 'He [Feuerbach] does not see how the sensuous world around him is, not a thing given direct from all eternity, ever the same, but the product of industry and the state of society; and indeed, in the sense that it is an historical product, the result of the activity of a whole succession of generations, each standing on the shoulders of the preceding one, de-

veloping its industry and its intercourse, modifying its social organisation according to the changed needs' (*The German Ideology*, p.35).

4. Easton and Guddat, eds. (1967) p.401.
5. This Hegelian concept signifies both abolition and transcendence, and was first employed by Marx in connection with the 'withering away' of the bourgeois state, cf. Avineri (1968), esp. pp.36-8, 208-12. The whole process of class conflict and proletarian revolution is described in *The Communist Manifesto* (1848), in Marx and Engels, ed. Feuer (1959), pp.1-41.
6. Cf. Marx's clear statement on the 'material elements of a complete revolution'; in Marx and Engels (1947); pp.29-30.
7. Bottomore, ed. (1964), p.166. (Marx, *Early Writings*).
8. Marx and Engels (1947) p.8, and esp. pp.16-7.
9. E.g. *ibid.*, pp.7, 14-15, 20-1, 29, 74-6; Marx and Engels (1959), pp.26-7, 43-4; Bottomore (1963), p.79 (*Capital*, I, 389).
10. Marx and Engels (1947), p.13.
11. *Ibid.*, pp.8-13, 43 sqq.
12. Class relationships are basically dichotomous and antagonistic, by definition (i.e. as they arise from the relations of production), but this antagonism is only realised in historical struggle through political action which requires a consciousness of a class's common interests on the part of its members, cf. the famous passage on the French peasants in *The Eighteenth Brumaire of Louis Bonaparte* (1852), in Feuer, ed. (1959) pp.338-9.
13. Marx, *The Poverty of Philosophy*, Moscow, n.d., p.197, cited in Avineri (1968) p.237.
14. Marx and Engels (1947), pp.67-9.
15. Marx (1859) Preface to *A Contribution to the Critique of Political Economy* in Marx and Engels, ed. Feuer (1959), pp.43-4.
16. Cf. Aron (1967), p.229. Weber borrowed the concept of charisma from Rudolf Sohm, a church historian and jurist.

Its literal meaning is 'gift of grace'.

17. Weber (1947), p.358.
18. *Ibid.*, p.359. Heroes in war or hunting, legal or medical wise men, magicians, shamans and prophets, demagogues like Kurt Eisner or exceptional intellectuals and artists, as well as saints and leaders of sects or orders like the Mormons or Franciscans, all possess the charismatic type of authority. Cf. Bendix: (1967).
19. Weber, (1948), pp.249-50 ('The sociology of charismatic authority', from *Wirtschaft und Gesellschaft* III, 9, pp. 753-7).
20. Weber (1966), p.59.
21. *Ibid.*, pp.124-5. Both the theoretical rationalism of merchants and artisans and the theoretical rationalism of intellectual strata have exerted a major influence on religious concepts of salvation, cf. Weber, (1948), pp. 279-80 ('The social psychology of the world religions', in *Gesammelte Aufsaetze zur Religionssoziologie*, Tubingen 1922-23, I, 237-68).
22. *Ibid.*, p.125.
23. Weber (1961), p.265.
24. Weber (1948), p.139 (*Science as a Vocation*).
25. Weber (1947), p.341; cf. Weber (1948), p.296 (*The Social Psychology of the World Religions*): ' "Traditionalism" in the following discussions shall refer to the psychic attitude-set for the habitual workaday and to the belief in the everyday routine as an inviolable norm of conduct. Domination that rests upon this basis, that is, upon piety for what actually, allegedly, or presumably has always existed, will be called "traditionalist authority".'
26. Weber (1961), p.55.
27. Weber (1952), IV/2, V/2-3, and esp. XI/1-3, 5, on prophecy.
28. Weber (1968), I/2, ch.5 ('Ethnic groups').
29. Cf. Antoni (1959), pp.165-7.
30. Weber (1966), p.96. Weber's point is that very different

48. Indeed, it is more appropriate to speak of Weber's method as one of tracing out the several causal chains which converge and intersect, in the explanation of a given phenomenon.

49. Weber (1949), p.57 (*'Objectivity' in social science and social policy*). Even the significance of 'problems' in research is largely decided on the basis of individual 'value-ideas' (*Wertideen*) derived from one's Weltanschauung, pp.56-60.

50. Weber (1948), p.152 (*Science as a Vocation*).

51. This is especially true of Weber's characterisation of religious influences on Indians and Israelites, but it also applies to those born into specific status groups, such as warrior castes or political officials, or ethnic minorities and sects (Parsees, Jains, Jews, Sikhs, Skoptzi, Pietists, as well as various Hindu sects are mentioned in Weber (1964) chs.6-7).

52. Cf. Marx and Engels (1947), pp.39-41.

53. Marx (1959), pp.320-2 (*The Eighteenth Brumaire of Louis Bonaparte*).

54. Marx and Engels (1947), pp.28-9.

55. Marx (1959), p.137 (*Capital*: Preface to first edition). The statement occurs in a methodological context: 'But here individuals are dealt with only insofar as they are personifications of economic categories, embodiments of particular class relations and class interests.' Nevertheless, the consequence of strict adherence to this method is the implicit subordination of individual action *as a causal influence* upon historical events and processes.

56. *Ibid.*, p.135.

57. *Ibid.*, pp.143-5. Marx's approval of the evolutionary framework (and even the organic analogy) reinforces the impression of immanentist growth, which admits neither of external intervention nor creative alternatives (except, of course, dissolution).

58. On the importance of this ethic for Marx's developmental-

ism, cf. Giddens (1971), chs.1-4, and esp. ch.14, p.212, and cf. the comments in Aron (1965), pp.177-9.

59. Marx, ed. Eastern and Guddat(1967), pp. 177 ff. (*Critique of Hegel's Philosophy of the State, 1843*).

60. Marx (1959), pp.43-4.

61. Marx (1970) I, ch.32.

62. Marx: *Werke* IV, 338-9 (Deutsche Brusseler Zeitung, 11 November 1847), cited in Avineri (1968), p.191. Cf. also the whole analysis of Marx's attitude to the French Revolution in Avineri's chapter, and Lichtheim (1961).

63. Cf. esp. the writings of Guerin, Soboul and Lefebvre.

64. Cobban (1965). This is not to say that demographic and economic (bread shortages) factors were not of vital importance in the years leading up to 1789; only that one cannot 'derive' the subsequent political struggles from them, and certainly not in the class form required by Marxist methodology.

65. Weber, ed. Gerth and Mills (1948), Introduction pp.46-50, and pp.77 ff.

66. Weber (1952), p.268.

67. *Ibid.*, pp.275, 278-9, 281-2, 292.

68. *Ibid.*, pp.277 ff.

69. Mommsen (1965), p.36, and for the influence on Weber of Nietzsche.

70. Cf. Markham (1954), chs.4, 6.

71. Weber (1948), p.125; cf. Wrong (1970), Introduction.

72. Marx: 'Letter to P.V. Annenkov', 28 Dec. 1846, in Karl Marx and Friedrich Engels, *Selected Correspondence*, Foreign Languages Publishing House, Moscow, n.d., cited in Banks (1972), pp.42-3. Cf. also Marx and Engels (1947), p.18.

73. Feuer (1959), pp.43-4. Hence the possibility of isolating 'the Asiatic, the ancient, the feudal, and the modern bourgeois methods of production as so many epochs in the progress of the economic formation of society'. For the evolutionary scheme itself, Marx and Engels were much

indebted to Morgan's recent work on the family, property and the State.

74. Marx: *Grundrisse der Kritik der politischen Ökonomie* (1857), pp.29-31 in McLellan (1971), pp.35-7.

75. *Ibid.*, pp.35-7, and in Marx and Engels (1974), pp.136-8; cf. also the Introduction to this selection of the writings of Marx and Engels on art and literature by S. Morawski, esp. pp.36 ff.

76. Weber (1948), p.341 (*Religious Rejections of the World and their Directions*).

77. *Ibid.*, p.342, and Marx and Engels (1974), pp.18-25, 59-65.

Chapter 7 Social theory and historical processes

1. Moore (1963), p.24. Moore's main argument is based upon the differences in type of social organisation which 'set different variables for analysing changes in patterns of action'. Here, however, the argument is based on the great range of variation in the relationships between often recurrent sequences of events, which compose patterns and units. Not only are there many kinds of event sequences and event clusters; they are also interrelated in so many ways, that a single overall 'theory' or framework could hardly cover many, let alone every one, of these interrelations and their effects.

2. On this explanatory inadequacy, cf. Smith (1973b), ch.3.

3. Cf. the essays in Eisenstadt (1970), Pt. III, and Nettl and Robertson (1968).

4. For a techno-economic Marxian version of anthropological evolutionism, cf. Harris (1968); a less Marxian perspective which marries a power theory to an evolutionary framework of stages of technological advance and surplus, is provided by Lenski (1966).

5. Cf. the criticisms of Marx's Europe-centred vision in Avineri (1969), Introduction, esp. pp.29-31 (*Karl Marx*

159

on *Colonialism and Modernisation*).

6. Cf. Fletcher (1974), pp.43-44. For some reasons for endogenism's appeal, cf. Smith (1973b), ch.7.
7. Little (1965).
8. Bastide (1961) and Balandier (1955) for such syncretism and the effects of colonialism in Black Africa.
9. On this last point, cf. Guessous (1967), pp.23-35.
10. Nisbet (1969), esp. ch.8, and (1970b), ch.5 ('History and sociology', originally published 1957). Cf. also Nisbet's (1967) comments on Stebbins's paper.
11. McNeill (1963).
12. Smelser (1959) and (1968).
13. Brinton (1952), who also traces a determinate sequences of stages through which the disease passes.
14. On the international context of nineteenth century revolutions, cf. Hobsbawm (1962), and the works cited by Palmer, Godechot and Rude. For twentieth century revolutions, cf. Seton-Watson (1951) and (1960); also Ulam (1960) on the uses of Marxism during incipient industrialisation, and Barrington Moore (1967) on different routes to modernity which tends to emphasise the agrarian basis within each society of its transformation.
15. Cf. Giddens (1971), ch.14; Wittfogel (1957), and Eisenstadt (1963).
16. Martins (1974), pp.278-9. Martins also uses the term 'inter-phenomena' to refer to 'trans-national' phenomena which are regular and normal, and which imply no asymmetry in their generation, such as the exogenists assume with their category of *in*truding (never *out*truding) events. Such phenomena, Martins adds, are constituted by 'mutual interactions', presumably between patterns or units. However, the very label for this category accepts, by implication, a world of analytically (at least) discrete phenomena (patterns or units, or both). 'Inter-phenomena' presumably stand (or are placed) between entities either as linking 'bridges' or simply as patterns of flow and inter-

action, more or less continuous and regular, but always symmetrical (cf. p.277). (In the latter case, especially, 'inter-phenomena' become the main tool and focus of research for the transunit 'interaction' category of change, outlined below.) The point remains that in arguing for the study of inter-phenomena, one inevitably assumes the possibility and utility of at least initial demarcations of units as a heuristic device, even if such scaffolding can be dismantled once understanding is attained.

17. Cf. Beloff (1954), Honour (1968) and, for a later period, Anderson (1972).
18. Cf. Daniel (1968) and especially Braidwood and Willey, eds. (1962).
19. For an introduction to the formative influences on early Florentine art, cf. Murray and Murray (1963). On the influences on Donatello, cf. Seymour, (1966). On the influence of religious orders and humanism, cf. Borsook (1960).
20. For a general introduction, cf. Honour (1968). On the impact of Rousseauan ideas for neo-classicism in literature and politics, cf. Kohn (1967). On historicism and neo-classicism, cf. Rosenblum (1967) and on the excavations and French revolutionary art, cf. Arts Council (1972).
21. Cf. the analysis in Smith (1973a), esp. pp.86-95.
22. On these influences, cf. Brandon (1967) and Carmichael (1966), chs.11-13.
23. Given that many of our historical documents are the work of intellectuals, care must be exercised in assessing their role as mediators (whether as propagandists or as creators of climates and potent ideas) of change. Nevertheless it is possible to provide considerable evidence for the importance of their contribution, both direct and indirect, even in premodern eras, and hence Shils's studies of intellectuals may well be applied to earlier times, cf. Shils (1960); also Eisenstadt (1972).

Bibliography

Almond, G. (1960) 'A functional approach to comparative politics', in G. Almond and J.S. Coleman, *The Politics of the Developing Areas*, Princeton University Press.

Almond, G. and
   Pye, L. eds. (1965) *Comparative Political Culture*, Princeton University Press.

Anderson, M.S. (1972) *The Ascendancy of Europe, 1815-1914*, Longman.

Andreski, S. ed. (1971) *Herbert Spencer: Structure, Function and Evolution*, Michael Joseph.

Antoni, C. (1959) *From History to Sociology*, trans. V. Hayden, Wayne State University Press.

Apter, D. ed. (1963) *Ideology and Discontent*, New York, Free Press.

Apter, D. (1965) *The Politics of Modernisation*, University of Chicago Press.

Apter, D. (1968) *Some Conceptual Approaches to the Study of Modernisation*, Prentice-Hall.

Aron, R. (1965, 1967) *Main Currents in Sociological Thought*, 2 vols, Penguin.

Arts Council of Great Britain (1972) *The Age of Neo-Classicism*, London (Shenval Press).

Avineri, S. (1968) *The Social and Political Thought of Karl Marx*, Cambridge University Press.

Avineri, S. ed. (1969) *Karl Marx on Colonialism and Modernisation*, Anchor Books.

Balandier, G. (1955) *Sociologie Actuelle de l'Afrique noire*, Presses Universitaires de France.

Banks, J.A. (1972) *The Sociology of Social Movements*, Macmillan.

Bastide, R. (1961) 'Messianisme et developpement economique et sociale', *Cahiers Internationaux de Sociologie* 31, 3-14.

Barnett, H.G. (1964) *Process and Pattern in Culture*, Aldine Publishing Co.

Barrington-Moore (1967) *Social Origins of Dictatorship and Democracy*, Allen Lane.

Beales, D. (1971) *The Risorgimento and the Unification of Italy*, Allen & Unwin.

Bellah, R. (1958) 'Religious Aspects of modernisation in Turkey and Japan', *American Journal of Sociology* 64, 1-5.

Bellah, R. (1959) 'Durkheim and history', *American Sociolgical Review* 24, 447-61.

Bellah, R. (1963) 'Reflections on the Protestant ethic analogy in Asia', *Journal of Social Issues* 19, 52-60.

Bellah, R. (1964) 'Religious evolution', *American Sociological Review* 29, 358-74.

Bellah, R. ed. (1965) *Religion and Progress in Modern Asia*, New York, Free Press.

Beloff, M. (1954) *The Age of Absolutism, 1660-1815*, Hutchinson.

Bendix, R. (1966) 'Tradition and modernity reconsidered', *Comparative Studies in Society and History* 9, 292-346.

Bendix, R. (1967) 'Reflections on charismatic leadership', *Asian Survey* 7, 341-52.

Binder, L. (1964) *The Ideological Revolution in the Middle East*, Wiley.

Birnbaum, N. (1953) 'Conflicting interpretations of the rise of capitalism: Marx and Weber', *British Journal of Sociology* 4, 125-41.

Bloch, M. (1965) *Feudal Society*, 2 vols, Routledge.

Boas, F. (1924) 'Evolution or diffusion?, *American Anthro-*

163

pologist **26**, 340-4.

Bock, K. (1963) 'Evolution, function and change', *American Sociological Review* **28**, 229-37.

Bock, K. (1964) 'Theories of progress and evolution', in Cahnmann and Boskoff (1964).

Bordes, F. (1968) *The Old Stone Age*, Thames & Hudson.

Borsook, E. (1960) *The Mural Painters of Tuscany*, Phaidon.

Boskoff, A. (1964) 'Recent theories of social change', in Cahnmann and Boskoff (1964).

Bottomore, T.B. ed. (1963) *Karl Marx, Selected Writings in Sociology and Social Philosophy*, Penguin.

Bottomore, T.B. ed. (1964) *Karl Marx, Early Writings*, Watts.

Bracher, K. (1973) *The German Dictatorship*, Penguin.

Braidwood, R. and
Willey, G. eds. (1962) *Courses towards Urban Life*, Aldine Publishing Company.

Brandon, S.G.F. (1967) *Jesus and the Zealots*, Manchester University Press.

Braudel, F. (1969) *Ecrits sur l'histoire*, Paris.

Brinton, C. (1952) *The Anatomy of Revolution*, revised edition, New York, Vintage.

Buckley, W. (1967) *Sociology and Modern Systems Theory*, Prentice-Hall.

Burn, A.R. (1973) *Alexander the Great and the Middle East*, revised edition, Penguin.

Burrow, J. (1966) *Evolution and Society*, Cambridge University Press.

Cahnmann, W. and
Boskoff, A. eds. (1964) *Sociology and History*, New York, Free Press.

Cancian, F. (1960) 'The functional analysis of change', *American Sociological Reveiw* **25**, 818-27.

Carmichael, J. (1966) *The Death of Jesus*, Penguin.

Carr, E.H. (1961) *What is History?*, Penguin.

Childe, V.G. (1936) *Man Makes Himself*, Watts.

Childe, V.G. (1942) *What Happened in History*, Penguin.

Childe, V.G. (1951) *Social Evolution*, Watts.

Clark, G. and
Piggott, S. (1965) *Prehistoric Societies*, Penguin.

Cobban, A. (1965) *The Social Interpretation of the French Revolution*, Cambridge University Press, Cambridge.

Coleman, J.S. *et al.* (1966) *Medical Innovation: a diffusion study*, Bobbs-Merrill.

Collins, D. *et al.* (1970) *Background to Archaeology*, Association for Cultural Exchange, Cambridge.

Comte, A. (1896) *The Positive Philosophy*, trans. H. Martineau, Bell.

Coulborn, R. ed. (1956) *Feudalism in History*, Princeton University Press.

Coulborn, R. (1959) *The Origin of Civilised Societies*, Princeton University Press.

Daniel, G. (1971) *The First Civilisations*, Penguin.

Deutsch, K.W. (1961) 'Social mobilisation and political development', *American Political Science Review* 55, 493-514.

Deutsch, K.W. (1966) *Nationalism and Social Communication*, 2nd edn, Wiley.

Dobzhansky, T. (1962) *Mankind Evolving*, Yale University Press.

Dumont, L. (1970) *Homo Hierarchicus*, Weidenfeld and Nicolson.

Durkheim, E. (1947a) *The Division of Labour in Society*, trans. Simpson, Chicago, Free Press.

Durkheim, E. (1947b) *Elementary Forms of the Religious Life*, trans. Swain, Chicago, Free Press.

Durkheim, E. (1962) *Socialism and St. Simon*, Collier Books.

Easton, L.D. and
Guddat, K.H. eds. (1967) *Writings of the Young Marx on Philosophy and Society*, Anchor Books.

Eckstein, H. ed. (1964) *Internal War*, Princeton University Press.

165

Eisenstadt, S.N. (1963) *The Political System of Empires*, New York, Free Press.

Eisenstadt, S.N. (1964a) 'Social change, differentiation and evolution', *American Sociological Review* **29**, 375-86.

Eisenstadt, S.N. (1964b) 'Modernisation and conditions of sustained growth', *World Politics* **16**, 576-94.

Eisenstadt, S.N. (1965) *Modernisation: protest and change*, Prentice-Hall.

Eisenstadt, S.N. (1968a) *The Protestant Ethic and Modernisation*, Basic Books.

Eisenstadt, S.N. (1968b) 'Some new looks at the problem of relations between traditional societies and modernisation', *Economic Development and Cultural Change* **16**, 436-50.

Eisenstadt, S.N. ed. (1970) *Readings in Social Evolution and Development*, Pergamon (essays: 'Social Change and Development' and 'Breakdowns of Modernisation' 1964 by S.N. Eisenstadt).

Eisenstadt, S.N. (1972) 'Intellectuals and tradition', *Daedalus* **101**, 1-19.

Eisenstadt, S.N. (1973) *Tradition, Change and Modernity*, Wiley.

Feuer, L.S. ed. (1959) *Marx and Engels: Basic Writings on Politics and Philosophy*, Anchor Books.

Finer, S.E. ed. (1966) *Vilfredo Pareto: Sociological Writings*, Pall Mall Press.

Fletcher, R. (1974) 'Evolutionary and developmental sociology, in Rex ed. (1974).

Frank, A.G. (1969) *Latin America: underdevelopment or revolution?*, New York, Monthly Review Press.

Frankfort, H. (1948) *Kingship and the Gods: a study of ancient Near Eastern religion as the integration of society and nature*, Chicago University Press.

Frankfort, H. (1956) *The Birth of Civilisation in the Near East*, Anchor Books.

Friedrich, C.J. (1962) *The Age of the Baroque, 1610-1660*, Harper and Row.

Garrod, D. and
  Clark J.G. eds. (1967) 'Primitive man in Egypt, Western Asia and Europe', *Cambridge Ancient History* I/1, Cambridge University Press.
Gellner, E. (1964) *Thought and Change*, Weidenfeld and Nicolson.
Gerth, H. and
  Mills, C.W. eds. (1948) *From Max Weber, Essays in Sociology*, Routledge.
Giddens, A. (1970) 'Marx, Weber and the development of capitalism', *Sociology* 4, 289-310.
Giddens, A. (1971) *Capitalism and Modern Social Theory*, Cambridge University Press.
Ginsberg, M. (1957) *Essays in Sociology and Social Philosophy*, I, Heinemann.
Godechot, J. (1965) *France and the Atlantic Revolution of the Eighteenth Century, 1770-1799*, trans. H.H. Rowen, New York, Free Press.
Goldthorpe, J., Lockwood. D. *et al.* (1968) *The Affluent Worker*, Cambridge University Press.
Gouldner, A. (1959) 'Reciprocity and autonomy in functional theory', in Gross, L. ed. *Symposium in Sociological Theory*, Harper and Row.
Gouldner, A. (1962) Introduction to Durkheim (1962).
Guessous, M. (1967) 'A general critique of equilibrium theory', in Moore and Cook (1967).
Gusfield, J. (1962) 'Mass society and extremist politics', *American Sociological Review* 7, 19-30.
Gusfield, J. (1967) 'Tradition and modernity: misplaced polarities in the study of social change', *American Journal of Sociology* 72, 351-62.

Hagen, E. (1962) *On the Theory of Social Change*, Dorsey.

Halpern, M. (1963) *The Politics of Social Change in the Middle East and North Africa*, Princeton University Press.

Harris, M. (1968) *The Rise of Anthropological Theory*, Columbia University Press.

Hay, D. (1961) *The Italian Renaissance in its Historical Background*, Cambridge University Press.

Herberle, R. (1951) *Social Movements: An Introduction to Political Sociology*, Appleton-Century-Crofts.

Heine-Geldern, R. (1956) 'The origin of ancient civilisations and Toynbee's theories', *Diogenes* 13, 81-99.

Hillier, B. (1968) *Art Deco*, Studio Vista.

Hobsbawm, E.J. (1962) *The Age of Revolution, 1789-1848*, Mentor Books.

Holborn, H. (1964) *A History of Modern Germany, 1648-1840*, Knopf.

Homans, G.C. (1964) 'Bringing men back in', *American Sociological Review* 29, 809-18.

Honour, H. (1968) *Neo-Classicism*, Penguin.

Horowitz, I.L. (1966) *Three Worlds of Development*, Oxford University Press, New York.

Hoselitz, B.F. (1960) *Sociological Factors in Economic Development*, Chicago, Free Press.

Hoselitz, B.F. and
Moore, W.E. eds. (1963) *Industrialisation and Society*, The Hague, Mouton.

Johnson, C. (1964) *Revolution and the Social System*, Stanford University Press.

Johnson, C. (1968) *Revolutionary Change*, University of London Press.

Kann, R.A. (1950) *The Multi-national Empire: nationalism and national reform in the Habsburg monarchy, 1848-1918*, Columbia University Press.

Kaufmann, Y. (1961) *The Religion of Israel*, Allen and Unwin.

Kautsky, J.H. ed. (1962) *Political Change in Underdeveloped Countries*, Wiley.

Kedourie, E. (1960) *Nationalism*, Hutchinson.

Kedourie, E. ed. (1971) *Nationalism in Asia and Africa*, Weidenfeld and Nicolson.

Kluckhohn, C. (1951) 'The study of culture', in D. Lerner and H.D. Lasswell, eds. *The Policy Sciences*, Stanford University Press, ch.5.

Kohn, H. (1967) *The Idea of Nationalism*, Collier Books.

Kornhauser, W. (1959) *The Politics of Mass Society*, Routledge.

Kroeber, A.L. (1952) *The Nature of Culture*, University of Chicago Press.

Kroeber, A.L. (1963) *Style and Civilisation*, University of California Press.

Kunkel, J.H. (1965) 'Values and behaviour in economic development', *Economic Development and Cultural Change* 13, 257-77.

Lagos, G. (1963) *International Stratification and Underdeveloped Countries*, University of North Carolina Press.

LaPiere, R.T. (1965) *Social Change*, McGraw-Hill.

Leiden, C. and
   Schmitt, K.M. (1968) *The Politics of Violence: Revolution in the Modern World*, Prentice-Hall.

Lenski, G. (1966) *Power and Privilege*, McGraw-Hill.

Lerner, D. (1958) *The Passing of Traditional Society*, Chicago, Free Press.

Levy, M. (1953) 'Contrasting factors in the modernisation of China and Japan', *Economic Development and Cultural Change* 2, 161-97.

Levy, M. (1966) *Modernisation and the Structure of Societies*, Princeton University Press.

Lichtheim, G. (1961) *Marxism*, Routledge.

Little, K. (1965) *West African Urbanisation*, Cambridge University Press.

Lowie, R. (1938) *A History of Ethnological Theory*, Harrap.

Luethy, H. (1964) 'Once again: Calvinism and capitalism', *Encounter* **22**, 26-38.

Markham, F. (1954) *Napoleon and the Awakening of Europe*, Penguin.

Martins. H. (1974) 'Time and theory in sociology', in Rex, ed. (1974).

Marx, K. (1953) *Grundrisse der Kritik der politischen Ökonomie*, Berlin translated as *Grundrisse*, Penguin, 1974.

Marx, K. (1963) *Selected Writings in Sociology and Social Philosophy*, ed. T.B. Bottomore and M. Rubel, Penguin.

Marx, K. (1964) *Early Writings*, ed. T.B. Bottomore, New York.

Marx, K. (1967) *Writings of the Young Marx on Philosophy and Society*, ed. L.D. Easton and K.H. Guddat, Anchor.

Marx, K. (1970) *Capital*, vol. 1, Lawrence and Wishart Books.

Marx, K. and

Engels, F. (1947) *The German Ideology*, Parts 1 and III. New York, International Publishers.

Marx, K. and

Engels, F. (1959) *Basic Writings on Politics and Philosophy*, ed. L.S. Feuer, Anchor Books.

Marx, K. and

Engels, F. (1974) *On Literature and Art*, ed. Lee Baxandall and Stefan Morawski, New York, International General.

McClelland, D.C. (1960) *The Achieving Society*, Van Nostrand.

McClelland, D.C. (1963) 'The achievement motive in economic growth', in Hoselitz and Moore, eds. (1963).

McCulley, B.T. *English education and the origins of Indian nationalism*, Gloucester, Mass., Smith.

McLellan, D.S. ed (1971) *Marx's Grundrisse*, Macmillan.

McNeill, W.H. (1963) *The Rise of the West*, University of Chicago Press.

Merritt, R.L. and
    Rokkan, S. eds. (1965) *Comparing Nations: The use of quantitative data in cross-national research*, Yale University Press.

Mommsen, W. (1965) 'Max Weber's political sociology and his philosophy of world history', *International Social Science Journal* 17, 35-45.

Moore, W.E. (1960) 'A reconsideration of theories of social change', *American Sociological Review* 25, 810-18.

Moore, W.E. (1963) *Social Change*, Prentice-Hall.

Moore, W.E. (1967) *Order and Change*, Wiley.

Moore, W.E. and
    Cook, R.M. eds. (1967) *Readings on Social Change*, Prentice-Hall.

Morgan, L. (1877) *Ancient Society*, London.

Murray, P. and
    Murray, L. (1963) *The Art of the Renaissance*, Thames and Hudson.

Nettl, J.P. and
    Robertson, R. (1968) *International Systems and the Modernisation of Societies*, Faber.

Nisbet, R.A. (1967) 'The irreducibility of social change: a comment on Professor Stebbins' paper', in Moore and Cook, eds. (1967).

Nisbet, R.A. (1969) *Social Change and History*, Oxford University Press.

Nisbet, R.A. (1970a) *The Social Bond*, Knopf.

Nisbet, R.A. (1970b) *Tradition and Revolt*, New York, Vintage Books Edition.

Nolte, E. (1965) *Three Faces of Fascism*, Holt, Rinehart and Winston.

Noth, M. (1960) *The History of Israel*, 2nd edn, A. and C. Black.

Palmer, R.R. (1959) *The Age of the Democratic Revolution*, Princeton University Press, vol.I.

Park, R.E. (1951) 'The City', *American Journal of Sociology* **20**, 584-6.

Park, R.E. (1960) *Race and Culture*, Free Press, Glencoe.

Parsons, T. (1960) *Structure and Process in Modern Societies*, Chicago, Free Press.

Parsons, T. (1961) 'Some considerations on the theory of social change', *Rural Sociology* **26**, 219-39.

Parsons, T. (1964) 'Evolutionary universals', *American Sociological Review* **29**, 339-57.

Parsons, T. (1965) 'Introduction', to Weber (1965).

Parsons, T. (1966) *Societies, Evolutionary and Comparative Perspectives*, Prentice-Hall.

Parsons, T. (1971) *The System of Modern Societies*, Prentice-Hall.

Pennock, J.R. ed. (1964) *Self-government in Modernising Societies*, Prentice-Hall.

Plumb, J.H. (1969) *The Death of the Past*, Penguin.

Pye, L. (1962) *Politics, Personality and Nation-Building: Burma's search for identity*, Yale University Press.

Pye, L. and
   Verba, S. (1965) *Political Culture and Political Development*, Princeton University Press.

Radcliffe-Brown, A.R. (1957) *A Natural Science of Society*, Chicago, Free Press.

Rex, J. ed. (1974) *Approaches to Sociology, An introduction to major trends in British sociology*, Routledge.

Rogers, E. (1962) *The Diffusion of Innovations*, New York, Free Press.

Rosenblum, R. (1967) *Transformations in late Eighteenth Century Art*, Princeton University Press.

Rostow, W. (1960) *The Stages of Economic Growth*, Cambridge University Press.

Rude, G. (1963) *Revolutionary Europe, 1783-1815*, Collins.

Sahlins, M. and
   Service E. (1960) *Evolution and Culture*, University of
   Michigan Press.
Seton-Watson, H. (1951) 'Twentieth century revolutions',
   The Political Quarterly **22**, 251-65.
Seton-Watson, H. (1960) *Neither War, Nor Peace*, Methuen.
Seymour, C. (1966) *Sculpture in Italy, 1400-1500*, Penguin,
   Pelican History of Art.
Shils, E. (1960) 'Intellectuals in the political development of
   the new states', *World Politics* **12**, 329-68.
Shils, E. (1961) 'Centre and periphery', in *The Logic of Personal Knowledge*, Routledge.
Shils, E. (1962) *Political Development in the New States*,
   The Hague, Mouton.
Smelser, N.J. (1959) *Social Change in the Industrial Revolution*, Routledge.
Smelser, N.J. (1962) *Theory of Collective Behaviour*, Routledge.
Smelser, N.J. (1968) *Essays in Sociological Explanation*,
   Prentice-Hall.
Smith, A.D. (1971) *Theories of Nationalism*, Duckworth.
Smith, A.D. (1973a) *Nationalism*: a trend report and bibliography, *Current Sociology* **21**, The Hague, Mouton.
Smith, A.D. (1973b) *The Concept of Social Change*, Routledge.
Smith, A.D. (1975) 'Social change and diffusionist theories',
   Philosophy of the Social Sciences **5**, 273-87.
Smith, G. Elliot (1932) *In the Beginning: the origin of civilisation*, Watts.
Spencer, H. (1896) *The Principles of Sociology* (1876),
   New York, Appleton.
Spencer, H. (1900) *First Principles* (1862), London.
Stebbins, G.L. (1967) 'Pitfalls and guideposts, in comparing
   organic and social evolution', in *Readings on Social Change*,
   ed. W.E. Moore and R.M. Cook, Prentice-Hall.

Steward, J. (1955) *Theory of Culture Change*, University of Illinois Press.

Steward, J. (1960) 'Evolution and social typology', in Tax, ed. (1960).

Stone, L. (1966) 'Theories of revolution', *World Politics* 18, 169-76.

Tarde, G. (1903) *The Laws of Imitation*, trs E.C. Parsons, Holt, Rinehart and Winston.

Tax, S. ed. (1960) *Evolution after Darwin*, University of Chicago Press.

Teggart, F. (1925) *Theory of History*, Yale University Press.

Thomas, W.I. and

Znaniecki, F. (1927) *The Polish Peasant in Europe and America*, Dover Publications.

Toynbee, A. (1954) *The Study of History*, Oxford University Press.

Trevor-Roper. H. (1961) *Jewish and Other Nationalisms*, Weidenfeld.

Tylor, E.B. (1865) *Researches into the Early History of Mankind and the Development of Civilisation*, Murray.

Tylor, E.B. (1881) *Anthropology*, London.

Tylor, E.B. (1889) 'On a method of investigating the development of institutions: applied to laws of marriage and descent', *Journal of the Royal Anthropological Institute* 18.

Tylor, E.B. (1891) *Primitive Culture* (1871), Murray.

Ulam, A. (1960) *The Unfinished Revolution*, Random House.

Urry, J. (1973) *Reference Groups and the Theory of Revolution*, Routledge.

Van den Berghe, P. (1963) 'Functionalism and the dialectic', *American Sociological Review* 28, 695-705.

Watt, W.M. (1961) *Islam and the Integration of Society*, Routledge.

Weber, M. (1930) *The Protestant Ethic and the Spirit of Capitalism*, Allen and Unwin.

Weber, M. (1947) *The Theory of Social and Economic Organisation*, ed. T. Parsons, Oxford University Press, paperback edition, Free Press of Glencoe, 1964.

Weber, M. (1948) *From Max Weber, Essays in Sociology*, ed. H. Gerth and C.W. Mills, Routledge.

Weber, M. (1949) *The Methodology of the Social Sciences*, New York, Free Press.

Weber, M. (1951) *The Religion of China*, Free Press of Glencoe.

Weber, M. (1952) *Ancient Judaism*, New York, Free Press.

Weber, M. (1958) *The Religion of India*, New York, Free Press.

Weber, M. (1961) *General Economic History*, Collier Books.

Weber, M. (1966) *The Sociology of Religion*, Methuen.

Weber, M. (1968) *Economy and Society*, ed. G. Roth, C. Wittich, 3 vols, New York, Bedminster Press.

Weber, M. (1970) *Max Weber*, ed. D. Wrong, Prentice-Hall.

Wertheim, W.F. (1974) *Evolution and Revolution*, Penguin.

White, L. (1949) *The Science of Culture*, New York, Grove Press.

Wilkinson, P. (1971) *Social Movement*, Macmillan.

Wilkinson, P. (1974) *Political Terrorism*, Macmillan.

Wittfogel, K. (1957) *Oriental Despotism*, Yale University Press.

Wittkower, R. (1973) *Art and Architecture in Italy, 1600-1750*, Penguin.

Wrong, D. ed. (1970) *Max Weber*, Prentice-Hall.

Index

Index

and evolutionary thought, 45
and mechanisms of change, 54
functions, 8, 35

Geertz, C., 47
generalised beliefs, 63, 64-5, 87
German Ideology, The (Marx), 95
Germany, 84, 85
Gilfillan, 89
Graebner, 43
Greece, 49, 52
growth images, 32-3, 54, 82,
    108-9, 125
guerilla networks, 71
Gumplowicz, 40

Hagen, E., 80
Hammurabi, 10
Harun al-Rashid, 10
Heberle, R., 89-90
Hegel, Georg W.F., 113
Hellenism, 127, 132
Heraclitus, 29
Hinduism, 52
historical change, 12, 14, 18
    and human choice, 27
    intrusion and selection in, 91-2
    in Marxist view, 96-7
    and neo-evolutionism, 63, 65,
      67-8
    and social evolutionism, 38
historical materialism, 111-12
historical rationality, 121
historical sociology, 1, 4, 135
    and achronological relativism,
      19
    evential, 17
Homer, 31
horizontal view of history, 40-1
Howarth, Charles, 89
human agency, 66, 67-9, 136
human choice, 25-8, 72-3, 89,
    100, 110; *see also* volun-
    tarism
humanity, 95-6
    evolution of, 46
hyper-diffusionism, 41-2

ideas, role of, 94-5, 105
ideologies, 83-7, 95, 100, 120,
    127, 137
immanent growth or change,
    assumption of, 62-3, 68, 117
    125, 127, 136
'immanentist', 108-9, 131
impact of external forces, 59-60,
    69, 91, 94, 124, 127-9, 132,
    137; *see also* exogenism
India, 6, 24, 52, 107, 109, 124
Indus civilisation, 48, 49
industrialisation, 30
industrialism, 59
Industrial Revolution, 62, 128
industrial societies, 8, 30, 38, 59
information networks, 74
innovation, 59, 62, 70, 91, 131
    cultural, 123
    large-scale, 88
    and modernisation, 76
    theory of, 78-83, 89-90, 121
institutions, 6, 127-8
intellectualism, 102, 120
intelligentsia, 84-5, 115, 135, 138
intergroup relations, 124
interior manipulation, 76
interpersonal relations, 76-7
interplay, interaction, *see* trans-
    unit interaction
intrasystemic change, 16
intrusions, 40, 41-2, 76, 83, 85-7,
    91-2, 110, 124-8*passim*,
    130, 132-3, 138
    charismatic, 101
invasionism, 42-3, 85
invention, 79, 81, 89
involution, 47
irrationality, 120-1, 136
Islam, 49, 52
isogenous model, 131
Israel, 52, 53, 103, 116-17
Italy, 31, 49, 58, 84, 107
Jacobins, 114
Japan, 6, 60
Java, 47
Jefferson, 51

180

Index

Toynbee, Arnold, 32
traditional societies
  and change, 7-8
  in evolution theory, 36-7
  and modernisation, 76-7
traits, 8-9
transformative potential, 57, 67, 69
transitional society, 75-7
transunit interaction, 71-2, 130-9
trends, 16, 17-18, 19, 123
  and active mode of change, 25-7
  and neo-evolutionism, 46
  in socio-economic change, 21
Trevor-Roper, H., 84, 87
Tylor, E.B., 36-7, 78

United Nations, 71
units, 8-10
  and change, 12-14, 15-16
  and exogenism, 131
  growth of, 35
  replacement of, 16
urbanisation, 74, 75, 91, 117, 129
utilitarian economics, 39

value-added methodology, 63, 65
value commitment, 136, 138
values, 100, 121
  modification of, 65
van den Berghe, P., 40
Vatican, 16, 118
Verba, S., 77
voluntarism, 105, 113, 121, 124, 133; *see also* human choice

wealth, passion for, 106
Weber, Max, 4, 6, 27, 39, 51, 54, 55-6, 57-8, 94-5, 136
  on ideology and revolution, 113, 116-19
  on irrationality, 119-21, 137
  on origins of capitalism, 106-13
  on origins of change, 100-5, 123-4, 128
Westermarck, 34
White, Leslie, 46
wholes, *see* entities
Wilkinson, P., 89
Wittfogel, K., 131
writing, 51

Znaniecki, 70